POSTER COLLECTION
EN VOGUE

32

Herausgegeben von / Edited by Bettina Richter

Essay von / by Elke Gaugele

MUSEUM FÜR GESTALTUNG ZÜRICH
PLAKATSAMMLUNG / POSTER COLLECTION

LARS MÜLLER PUBLISHERS

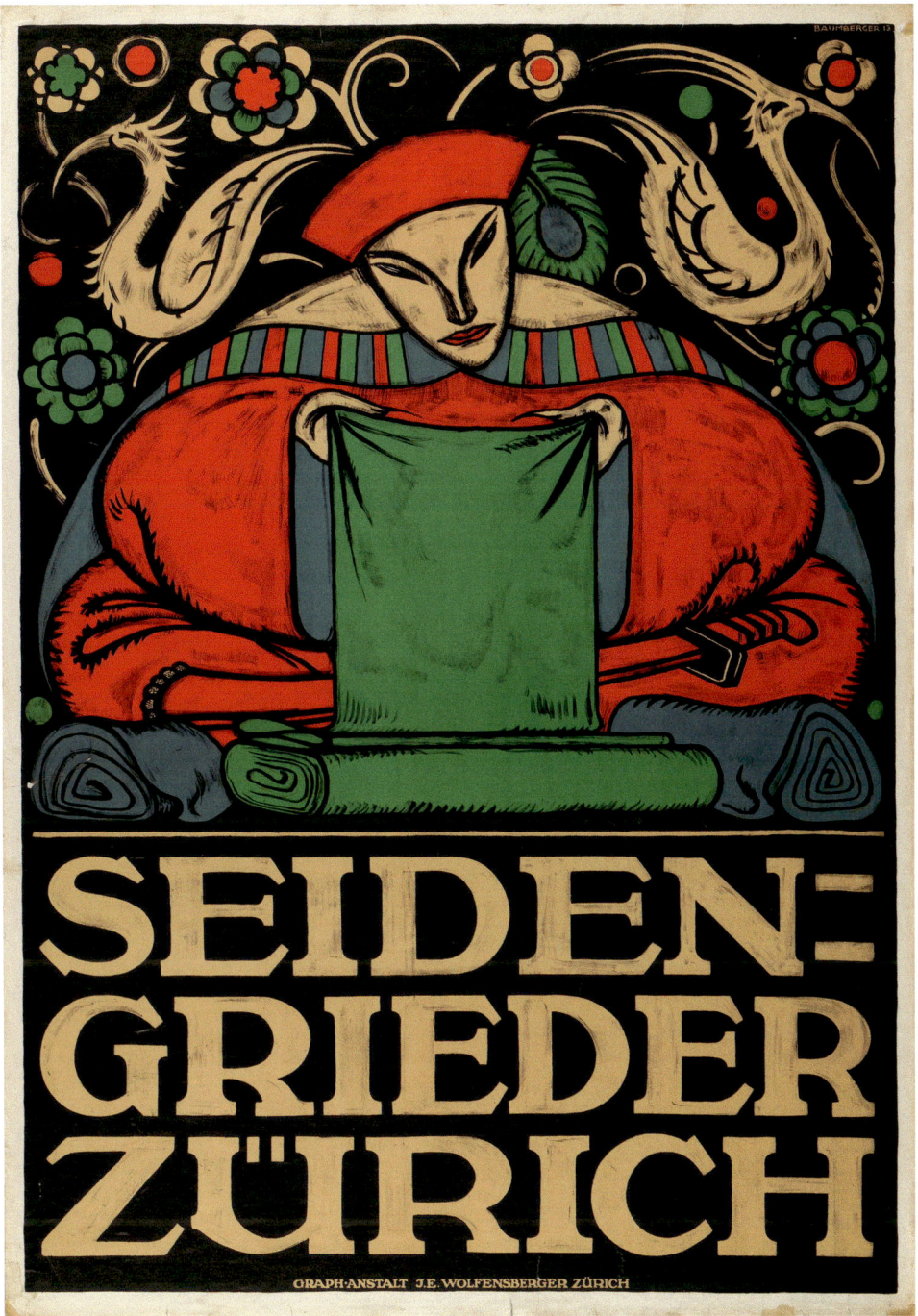

1 **Otto Baumberger**
Seiden-Grieder
1913

VORWORT

Die bekannten Verheissungen der Werbung, dem Alltag zu entfliehen, Glück und Schönheit zu erfahren, erleben im Modeplakat eine zusätzliche Akzentuierung – geht es doch um das absolute Versprechen einer neuen Identität einzig durch das Tragen bestimmter Kleidung. Ist das Plakat immer auch Zeitzeugnis, so spiegeln sich im Modeplakat gängige Moralvorstellungen, aktuelle Schönheitsbilder und gesellschaftliche Verhältnisse in besonderer Weise.

Als Gattung kommt das Modeplakat in den 1920er-Jahren auf. Zunächst sind es Bekleidungsgeschäfte, die mit dem Medium die Aufmerksamkeit suchen. Ihre Botschaft zielt in jenen frühen Jahren auf soziale Distinktion: Die gehobene Gesellschaft ist das Zielpublikum von Seiden-Grieder und PKZ. Beste Qualität und Verarbeitung werden beworben. Der legendäre Mantelkragen von Otto Baumberger aus dem Jahr 1923 steht exemplarisch für die Werbeabsicht jener Zeit. Werden Kunden in den Blick gerückt, sind es nicht Individuen mit eigenwilligem Kleidungsstil, sondern Stellvertreter eines gut situierten, angepassten Bürgertums. Nach dem Zweiten Weltkrieg findet parallel zur Verbreitung von Markenartikeln und Selbstbedienungsläden ein Demokratisierungsprozess statt: Mode wird mehr und mehr zum persönlichen Statement und Lifestyle. Neue Zielgruppen und Subkulturen werden angesprochen. Qualität als Verkaufsargument rückt in den Hintergrund; vielmehr geht es nun darum, mit Mode ein Image zu kreieren und den Individualismus der Nachkriegsgesellschaft zu bedienen. Die lustvolle Selbstdarstellung über ausgesuchte Kleidung, aber auch Mode als Ausdruck des Protests werden zunehmend ein Thema. Aufwendige fotografische Inszenierungen entwerfen die passenden Lebenswelten, erzählen Geschichten, funktionieren als emotionaler Appell. Die sich wandelnden Geschlechterrollen ebenso wie neue körperliche Freiheiten zeigen sich exemplarisch in Jeans-Plakaten: Der Aufstieg der Arbeiterhose zur hippen Unisex-Bekleidung ab den späten 1950er-Jahren führt zu innovativen, frechfrivolen oder auch sinnlich-poetischen Werbebildern. Im Zeitalter der Aufmerksamkeitsökonomie sucht Oliviero Toscani für seine Benetton-Kampagnen der 1990er-Jahre nach neuen Inhalten in der Modewerbung. Seine Plakate wollen einen Skandal provozieren und führen zu heftigen ethischen Diskussionen in der Branche und darüber hinaus. Aktuell signalisieren weniger normative Männer- und Frauenbilder den Aufbruch in neue Zeiten. Doch müssen die Suche nach Individualität und die Sehnsucht nach kollektiver Zugehörigkeit hier ebenfalls ständig neu ausbalanciert werden.

Modeplakate aus hundert Jahren erzählen im Zeitraffer auch eine Geschichte der Werbung und ihrer Strategien. Das Spiel mit Konvention und Provokation, mit Klischees und Tabubrüchen entfaltet hier seine besondere Wirkung. Mal werden gesellschaftliche Werte und Geschlechterrollen zementiert, mal widerlegt. Und stärker als in jeder anderen Plakatgattung ist das Publikum Teil der Kommunikation und erlebt das eigene Selbst im Wechselbad von Dekonstruktion und Neuerschaffung.

Bettina Richter

FOREWORD

Fashion posters, with their firm pledges that we can take on a new identity simply by wearing certain clothes, heighten advertising's familiar promises of happiness, beauty, and an escape from everyday life. While posters always testify to their own era, fashion posters provide a very particular reflection of established moral conventions, current beauty ideals, and social circumstances.

The fashion poster emerged as a genre in the 1920s. Initially, clothing stores sought to attract attention using this medium. In those early years, their messages highlighted social distinctions: the upper classes were the target audience for Seiden-Grieder and PKZ. Advertising emphasized outstanding quality and workmanship. The era's promotional goals are exemplified by Otto Baumberger's legendary coat collar from 1923. When clients take center stage, they epitomize the conformist, well-to-do bourgeoisie rather than figuring as individuals with their own particular style. After the Second World War, the situation grew more democratic as branded goods and self-service stores spread: fashion increasingly became a personal statement and lifestyle choice. New target groups and subcultures were addressed. Quality took a back seat as a sales argument as the focus shifted to creating an image through fashion and serving individualism in postwar societies. Enthusiastic self-presentation with hand-picked outfits played a growing role, as did fashion as an expression of protest. Elaborate photographic stagings sketch out the corresponding lifeworlds while also recounting narratives and appealing to emotions. Jeans posters offer prime examples of shifting gender roles and new physical freedoms: from the late 1950s, these now hip unisex trousers, originally worn by manual laborers, gave rise to advertising images that were innovative, cheekily frivolous, and sensuously poetic. In the attention economy age, Oliviero Toscani hunted out new content in fashion advertising for his 1990s Benetton campaigns. Aiming to provoke and scandalize, his posters sparked heated ethical discussions in the industry and beyond. Today, less normative images of men and women are signaling the dawn of a new era. Striking a balance between the quest for individuality and the longing to belong nevertheless remains vital.

Fashion posters spanning a hundred years tell the story of advertising and its strategies as if in a time-lapse film. They highlight the experimentation with conventions and provocation, with clichés and violated taboos. Social values and gender roles are sometimes reinforced, sometimes rebutted. More than in any other poster genre, the audience forms part of the communication process and experiences its own identity in alternating deconstruction and re-creation.

Bettina Richter

2 **Niklaus Stoecklin**
PKZ
1934

la moda
si diffonde con
*la*Rinascente

3 **Lora Lamm**
La moda si diffonde con la Rinascente
1959

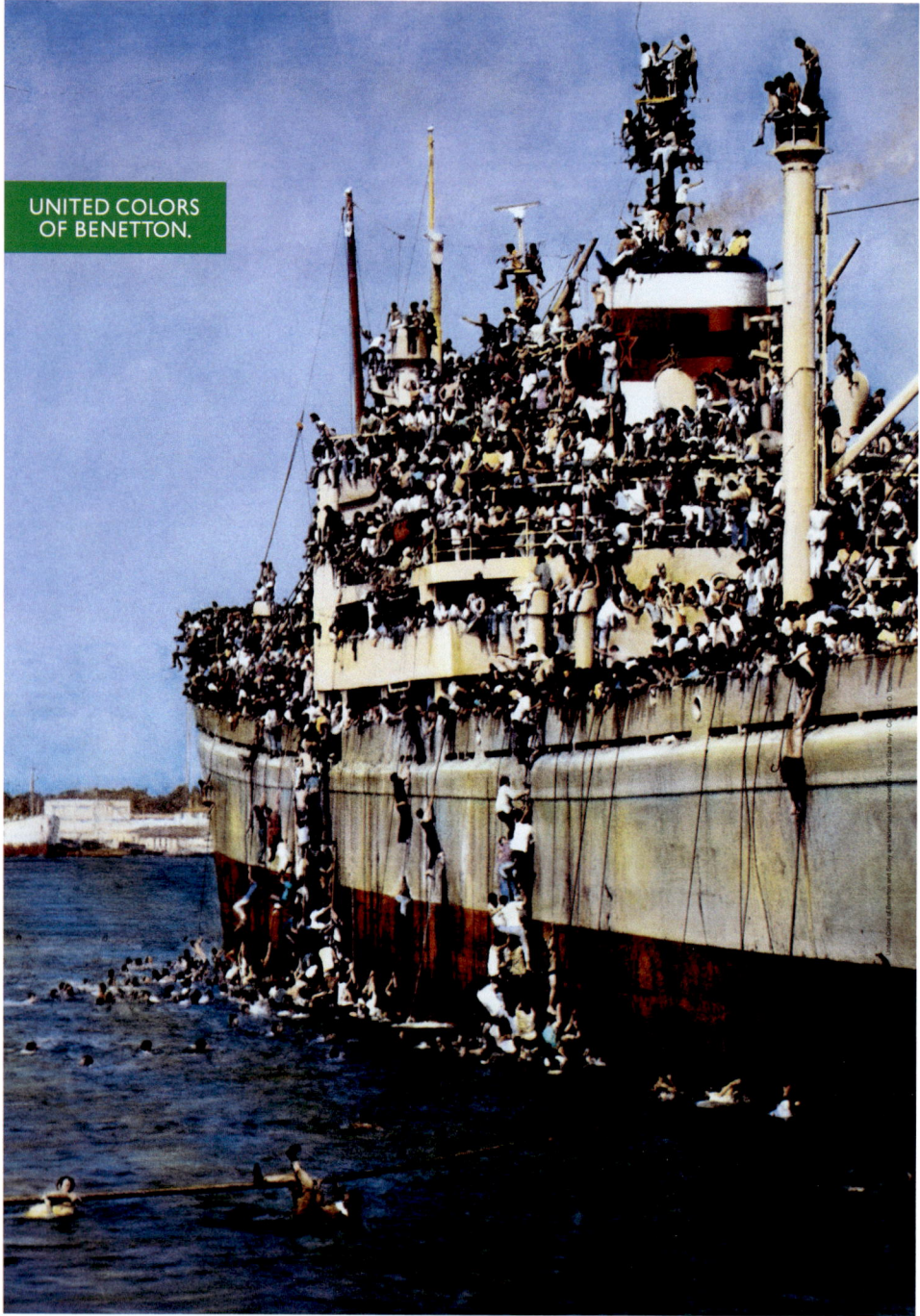

UNITED COLORS
OF BENETTON.

4 **Oliviero Toscani**
United Colors of Benetton.
1992

mountain

mountain
summit
pass
spur
ridge
peak
ridge
glacier
plateau
crevasse
slope
gorge/
ravine
moraine
waterfall
valley

dictionary
Mind of Telepathy

Supring-Summer 2010
Ladies wear and
Accessories

5 **Rikako Nagashima**
Dictionary / Mind of Telepathy
2010

energy project group

SISLEY

SISLEY.COM

6 **Anonym**
Sisley
2002

READING FASHION MOODS: EINE VISUELLE GESCHICHTE DER MODE

Elke Gaugele

Mode ist ein System, das Kleidung medial in die «Sprache der Mode»[1] übersetzt. Seit der Moderne spielt die Produktion von Kleidung als Mode vermittelt durch Bilder, Medien, Werbung und Plakate, die sich hier zu einer visuellen Geschichte der Mode aus mehr als einhundert Jahren verdichten, eine Schlüsselrolle. Modemedien gestalten Zeit und Raum und machen gerade durch ihren Wandel Zeitgenossenschaft ästhetisch erfahrbar. Als Paradigma für Kultur, Fortschritt und für das Neue schlechthin definierte Mode im kolonialen Machtgefüge der Moderne Superiorität und die Erscheinungsbilder des «zivilisierten» Westens. Teil dessen sind auch Verfahren kultureller Aneignung, der ästhetischen Einverleibung eines exotisch «Anderen», wie es ein orientalistisches Jugendstilplakat 1 veranschaulicht, welches diese Publikation eröffnet. Mode gestaltet bis heute am Körper den Übergang «vom Sinnlichen zum Sinn»[2], kommuniziert Leitbilder, Werte und Normen von Identität, Ethnizität, Gender, Klasse und Nation. In Zeiten digitaler Modemedien, boomender afrikanischer Fashion Cities und Modest Fashion Weeks in Dubai, Jakarta und London formt Mode globale Hierarchien und Ökonomien – und damit verbunden Individualität und Gemeinschaft.

KLEIDUNG UND MODE

Kleidung und Mode sind unterschiedliche Konzepte und Ökonomien des Mehr- und Sachwerts der Bekleidung. Dies spiegeln bereits die frühen Plakate wider. Als Thorstein Veblen um die Jahrhundertwende von der «Kleidung als Beweis der Zahlungsfähigkeit» sprach, bezog er sich darauf, dass Kleider ihren kommerziellen Wert aus der Tatsache schöpfen, dass sie als Mode den Konsumentinnen und Konsumenten Schönheit und zusätzlich einen verlockenden Mehrwert versprechen.[3] Doch betonen die Plakate noch bis in die Nachkriegszeit hinein, dass es ihnen explizit um Kleidung und um das Kleiden geht. In einer Zeit, in der die Kaufhäuser die serienmässige Produktion von Anzügen und Konfektionsware in genormten Kleidergrössen übernahmen, beharren sie darauf, dass Kleidung zunächst nicht Mode werden, sondern explizit Kleidung sein möchte. Slogans wie «die besten Stoffe der Welt» (PKZ) 12, «erstklassige Verarbeitung» (Tuch AG) 14 oder «durable» 31 betonen die «Gute Form», die dauerhafte Qualität, das Handwerk und damit den Sachwert der Bekleidung. Die Distanz und neutrale Haltung der Plakate gegenüber dem Modischen zeugen von den feinen Unterschieden und von einer Distinktion, die Klasse, Stil und vielleicht darüber hinaus auch die gesamte Nation aus dem Prinzip der Schlichtheit, Sachlichkeit und Männlichkeit heraus verstanden haben möchte. Elegante Männer(-gruppen) in dunklen, auch gestreiften oder karierten Anzügen, in langen Mänteln und mit Hüten 16–18 verbildlichen die Uniformierung der modernen Männlichkeit. Die Plakatgestalter zeichnen dabei ästhetische Zusammenhänge zwischen Anzügen, Mänteln und Uniformen, zwischen Wirtschaft und Militär. Vergleichsweise marginal vertreten sind demgegenüber Frauen. Dass Mode in der Moderne ein Produkt der Haute Couture und ein Zeitphänomen

---

1 Roland Barthes [1967], *Die Sprache der Mode.* Frankfurt a. M. 1985.
2 Ebd., S. 288.
3 Thorstein Veblen [1899], *Theorie der feinen Leute. Eine ökonomische Untersuchung der Institutionen,* Frankfurt a. M. 2007, S. 164.

repräsentativer Weiblichkeit war, dass sie Frauen zugeschrieben und von ihnen getragen wurde, spiegeln die Plakate bis in die Nachkriegszeit hinein kaum wider. Die wenigen Frauenfiguren repräsentieren Luxus in Gestalt eines exotisch-animalischen «Anderen»: expressionistisch-theatralisch im Pelz 20 oder in der voluminösen, an den Couturier Paul Poiret angelehnten Wickelrobe der Zürcher Firma Seiden-Grieder 9. Erst in den 1950er-Jahren treten Frauen verstärkt im Modeplakat in Erscheinung, so beispielsweise in der Werbung für das innovative Mailänder Warenhaus La Rinascente, die von Max Huber und Lora Lamm gestaltet wurde. Mit ihnen betritt auch die «Sprache der Mode» für industriell gefertigte Konfektion 44 die Bühne und definiert dabei deren Wirkungsbereiche: «La Moda 1960 – per la città, i viaggi, la professione» 43.

VOM HANDWERK ZUR GLOBAL FACTORY
«Handwerk hat hohe Geltung» – unter diesem Motto zeigt PKZ 1961 die Figur eines Firmenchefs mit Nadel und Faden im Schneidersitz 13. Höchstpersönlich näht der «Chef» im weissen Hemd mit Krawatte, bedacht durch seine Brille blickend, in Handarbeit das glänzende Innenfutter ein. Obwohl zum Zeitpunkt dieser Inszenierung des Gestalters Sandro Bocola und des Fotografen Max Emil Buchmann bereits mehr als 1000 Näherinnen und überwiegend weibliche Angestellte für PKZ in zwei Fabriken in Zürich und Massagno und in 15 Filialen in allen grossen Schweizer Städten arbeiteten, wirkt die Nadelarbeit auf dem Plakat im Zeitraffer der seinerzeit beginnenden Globalisierung wie eine Geste kontemplativer Ruhe. Bereits fünf Jahre später wurden für das Unternehmen erste Probleme spürbar: Aufgrund steigender Mieten, Kapitalkosten und Zollschranken wurde 1974 denn auch die Schweizer Textilfabrikation eingestellt und die Produktion ins Ausland – heute China, Indien sowie (südost-)europäische Länder – ausgelagert. 1978 markierte die erste H&M-Filiale in der Schweiz die Wende zur Fast Fashion. Als Reaktion auf das Outsourcing der Textilproduktion in Niedriglohnländer, Freihandelszonen und Sweatshops – Betriebe mit langen Arbeitszeiten, niedriger Bezahlung und schlechten gesundheitlichen Bedingungen – wurden nach 1989 nationale Kampagnen für Saubere Kleidung in mehr als 15 europäischen Ländern gegründet, ein zivilgesellschaftlicher Protest gegen die neue Kalkulation von Mode: die Verschiebung des Waren- zugunsten des Imagewerts. Die steigende Bedeutung von Bildern und Logos für die Einnahmen der Konzerne führt zu wachsenden Werbeetats für Stars und Supermodels. Sie charakterisieren die Ära des Brandings, in der beschleunigte Modezyklen zu Niedriglöhnen produziert werden. Im Übergang zum digitalen Zeitalter vergrössern sich im Wettbewerb um die Aufmerksamkeit der Konsumentinnen und Konsumenten nicht nur die Plakatflächen, sondern erhöht sich auch die Intensität jener visuellen Kampagnen, die mit einer Flut an perfekten Körperbildern fortan den Körper zur Mode machen. Die ausgewählten Plakate spiegeln den Aufstieg grosser multinationaler Marken seit den 1980er-Jahren wider, deren Logos in den nächsten Jahrzehnten nicht nur auf dem menschlichen Oberkörper, sondern auch im öffentlichen Raum expandieren: von Luxusmodemarken wie Hugo Boss, Versace

oder Calvin Klein bis hin zu den Jeansmarken Diesel, Levi's, und Lee Cooper oder dem Label Sisley der italienischen Benetton Group 101–104, 111–130.

MODE UND ETHIK

«Empty your closets» – «I want my clothes back» – mit grossen schwarzen Lettern, die den Körper des nackten Luciano Benetton überziehen, wirbt der Konzern 1993 für ein Clothing Redistribution Project: Er ruft dazu auf, Altkleider für die Schweizer Caritas, das Rote Kreuz und den Roten Halbmond zu spenden 115. Mit dieser Marketingkampagne versucht Oliviero Toscani – der von 1982 bis 2000 und von 2017 bis 2020 für Benetton arbeitete – dem Vorwurf entgegenzuwirken, mit den Tragödien anderer den globalen Ausbau und Gewinn der Marke voranzutreiben, der auf seine vorausgegangenen «Schockkampagnen» hin laut wurde 4. In der Tradition der dokumentarischen *concerned photography* [4], die humanitäre Impulse setzt und Fotografie als Medium zur Veränderung der Welt versteht, begann Toscani 1992 damit, aktuelle Pressefotos für die Benetton-Werbung zu appropriieren.[5] Statt Supermodels und Celebrities zu engagieren, produzierte er sozialkritische Werbeplakate zu gesellschaftlichen Themen wie Rassismus, Behinderung, Homosexualität, Aids oder die Todesstrafe. Unter dem Logo des Konzerns zirkulierte fortan ein stark beachtetes – und bis vor Gericht umstrittenes – Spektrum an globalisierungskritischen Dokumentarfotografien, die Missstände anprangerten. Verzahnt mit den neoliberalen Globalisierungsstrategien des Konzerns, spiegelt diese Bild- und Imageproduktion jenen Widerspruch wider, den Luc Boltanski und Ève Chiapello als «neuen Geist des Kapitalismus» benannt haben: «Wie lässt sich im Sinne des Gemeinwohls die Teilnahme am kapitalistischen Unternehmen rechtfertigen und im Hinblick auf die Vorwürfe der Ungerechtigkeit die Art verteidigen, mit der der Prozess geleitet wird?»[6] Diese Paradoxie ist jedoch charakteristisch für die gesamte Modeentwicklung im Anthropozän und Mitauslöser für den Ethical Turn in der Mode des 21. Jahrhunderts, infolgedessen immer mehr Designerinnen und Designer wie Vivienne Westwood, Bruno Pieters, Christopher Raeburn oder Stella McCartney begannen, als Umweltaktivistinnen und Umweltaktivisten aufzutreten. Auch die Diesel-Kampagnen «Nature – Love It While It Lasts» (2004) 75 und «Global Warming Ready» (2007) 125 oder jene von Levi's (2008) 99, 100 dokumentieren diese Entwicklung. Mit dem Plakat «United Victims of Benetton» forderten Aktivistinnen und Aktivisten Entschädigungen für die Opfer und Überlebenden des Rana-Plaza-Unglücks, bei dem im April 2013 in Bangladesch mehr als 1100 Arbeiterinnen und Arbeiter getötet und weitere Tausende verletzt worden waren. Der Benetton-Konzern, der wie zum Beispiel auch Primark, Lee Cooper, Zara oder Mango Textilien aus dem Rana Plaza bezogen hatte, unterzeichnete erst 2015 den Global Compact der UN und verpflichtete sich (freiwillig), Menschen- und Arbeitsrechte zu wahren sowie Umweltschutz zu garantieren.

KUNST ALS SPRACHE DER MODE

Konzeptionelle Ansätze in der Mode existieren schon seit dem frühen 20. Jahrhundert – Elsa Schiaparellis ikonischer Schuh-Hut etwa inspirierte Ende der 1950er-Jahre

4 Cornell Capa (Hg.), *The Concerned Photographer. The Photographs of Werner Bischof, André Kertész, Robert Capa, Leonard Freed, David Seymour («Chim»), Dan Weiner,* New York 1968.
5 Siehe auch Bettina Richter, «Zeitgenössische ‹Bilderstürmer›», in: Museum für Gestaltung Zürich, Bettina Richter (Hg.), *Help!,* Poster Collection 20, Baden 2009, S. 64–65.
6 Luc Boltanski, Ève Chiapello, «Die Arbeit der Kritik und der normative Wandel», in: Christoph Menke, Juliane Rebentisch (Hg.), *Kreation und Depression. Freiheit im gegenwärtigen Kapitalismus,* Berlin 2019, S. 18–37, hier S. 20.

ein polnisches Modeplakat 33. Surrealistische Motive, Wortbilder und dadaistische Collagetechniken durchziehen die Modeplakate des 20. Jahrhunderts. Doch während Mode und Kunst in der Theorie der Moderne noch auf unterschiedlichen Zeitachsen positioniert sind und Charles Baudelaire die Kunst als das «Ewige und Unverwandelbare»[7] und die Mode als «das Vergängliche, das Flüchtige, das Zufällige»[8] betrachtete, sind sich deren Dynamiken im Verlauf der Postmoderne immer näher gekommen.

Als Avantgarde der «Japanese Fashion Revolution» kooperierten Issey Miyake 81–84, Yōhji Yamamoto und Rei Kawakubo seit den 1970er-Jahren bei der Entwicklung ihrer Kollektionen genauso wie beim Marketing und der Imageproduktion mit Künstlerinnen und Künstlern sowie Museen. Minimalistisch in White Cube Fashion Stores präsentiert, forderten deren monochrome, skulpturale, asymmetrische, oft unfertig oder gebraucht wirkende weite Looks gängige Schönheitsvorstellungen und auch Tragegewohnheiten heraus. Die Pariser Modeschauen der Japanerinnen und Japaner beeinflussten in den 1980er-Jahren nicht nur Martin Margiela und die Antwerp Six, sondern trugen massgeblich zur Formierung einer neuen Ära der Conceptual Fashion bei. An konzeptuellen Zugängen, das Modesystem ästhetisch zu de- und rekonstruieren, arbeitete seit Mitte der 1990er-Jahre eine weitere Generation Modeschaffender, die unter dem Diktum «Not in Fashion!» als avantgardistische Gegenbewegung zur Modeindustrie antrat und seither nicht nur das Verhältnis von Mode und Kunst, sondern auch dasjenige von Design und Modekritik sowie von Mode und Anti-Mode neu justiert hat. Zeitgleich begann ein regelrechtes Co-Branding des Mode- und Kunstsystems, im Zuge dessen Luxusmarken nicht nur zunehmend mit Kunstschaffenden kooperierten, sondern auch als Sponsoren von Ausstellungen und Biennalen auftraten. Während die Zahl der Designerinnen und Designer, die im Kontext zeitgenössischer Kunst gezeigt wurden, stieg und Modemarken wie Prada eigene Museen für ihre Kunstsammlungen eröffneten, wurde auch für viele Künstlerinnen und Künstler, wie etwa das niederländische Fotografenduo Inez van Lamsweerde und Vinoodh Matadin, die Mode zum form- und inhaltgebenden Prinzip. In Kooperation mit dem Kunst- und Designduo M/M (Paris) produzierten sie 2001 unter dem Titel «The Alphabet» ein «A to Z of beauty» 65–68, bei dem die Fotografien der Models zu einer «weiblichen» Typografie zurechtgeschnitten wurden. Für Issey Miyake hatte Masaaki Hiromura bereits 1990 die Sprache der Mode mit den Lettern der Kunst buchstabiert 21–23.

VISUELLER POP
Die japanischen Plakate lesen sich wie ein Moodboard für den steilen Aufstieg Tokios zum Zentrum der Mode und der Streetstyles. In den 1980er-Jahren erzeugten sie den visuellen Soundtrack für den Übergang vom New Wave zum sogenannten «Designer-and-Character»-Boom, dem ersten avantgardistischen japanischen Modetrend. Teil dieser Szene war Makoto Saito, der – auch angeregt durch amerikanische Pop-Ästhetik – Plakate ohne Slogans produzierte, unter anderem für die Modelabels Ba-Tsu, Alpha Cubic, Jun Men und Kind Wear 85–98. Auch japanische Fast-Fashion-

---

7 Charles Baudelaire [1860], «Der Maler des modernen Lebens», in: ders., *Aufsätze zur Literatur und Kunst 1857–1860, Sämtliche Werke/Briefe,* Bd. 5, hg. von Friedhelm Kemp und Claude Pichois, München 1989, S. 213–258, hier S. 225.
8 Ebd., S. 215, Anm. 5.

Brands wie das Teenager-Wäschelabel Une nana cool 74 griffen diesen Trend auf. Als Pioniere des japanischen «Fashion Building» und Trendsetter für Jugendkulturen forcierten neue grosse Einkaufszentren das Crossover von Kunst, Mode und Popkultur. Das landläufig als Fashion-Panoptikum bezeichnete Laforet Harajuku 62, 64, 72 eröffnete 1978 als grosser Department-Komplex mit rund 150 Läden und einem Museum. Shi-buya Parco betrieb seit 1977 eine eigene Trend-Watching-Agentur für Street-Fashion-Marketing 73. Auch Vivre beauftragte in den 1990er-Jahren Masami Shimizu 58, 61, 63 und Jun Shibata 57 mit Plakaten im Stil der Konzeptkunst oder in den 2000er-Jahren die Popkünstlerin Nagi Noda 71 für ein schrilles Fitnessplakat, auf dem sie mit ironischem Augenzwinkern – nicht zuletzt auf Jeff Koons – das Bodystyling von Frau und Pudel parallelisiert. Höhere Sphären visualisiert demgegenüber die Grafik- und Textildesignerin Rikako Nagashima für Dictionary, indem sie das Foto des Models in «Mind of Telepathy» mit der künstlerischen Kartografie einer Berglandschaft überzeichnet 5.

Vom Bild des Hippies im Zustand der Erleuchtung über die Kommodifizierung des Punk und Kawaii-Stils hin zu Normcore und Instagram-Posen haben sich Jugendkulturen global als visuelle Popscapes entwickelt. Auch die Boutiquen und Labels des Schweizer Modebooms der 1970er- und 1980er-Jahre warben mit popkulturellen Collage- und Siebdruckästhetiken: Punch 107, Dschingis 32, Thema Selection, Drake Store 106, Löw Boutique 47–50 oder Au père et fils 108. An der Jeans entfaltet sich die globale Sprache jugendkultureller Rebellion mit Bildern von Körpern, Geschlechtern und Begehren. Sie sind, wie Erving Goffman in Geschlecht und Werbung ausführt, durch Rangordnungen und Rituale der Unterordnung strukturiert.[9] Die 1970er-Jahre kreisen um die Natursehnsucht heterosexueller Paare – im Boot am einsamen Strand 37 oder als Tarzan und Jane im Dschungel 109 – und verhandeln den Topos der Freiheit an nackten Oberkörpern (Lee Cooper, 1971) 38. Moden formen Sexualitäten: durch Unisex-Jeans genauso wie durch hyperreale sexistische Bilder der «Traumjeans» 101. Im Übergang zum 21. Jahrhundert hat die Mode ein breites Spektrum queerer LGBTQ+-Identitäten produziert, so posiert etwa der muskulöse Cowboy als Repräsentant der Gay Community mit einladenden Gesten zu Lou Reeds Song-Slogan «On the Wild Side» 130.

9 Erving Goffman [1979], Geschlecht und Werbung, Frankfurt a. M. 1981.

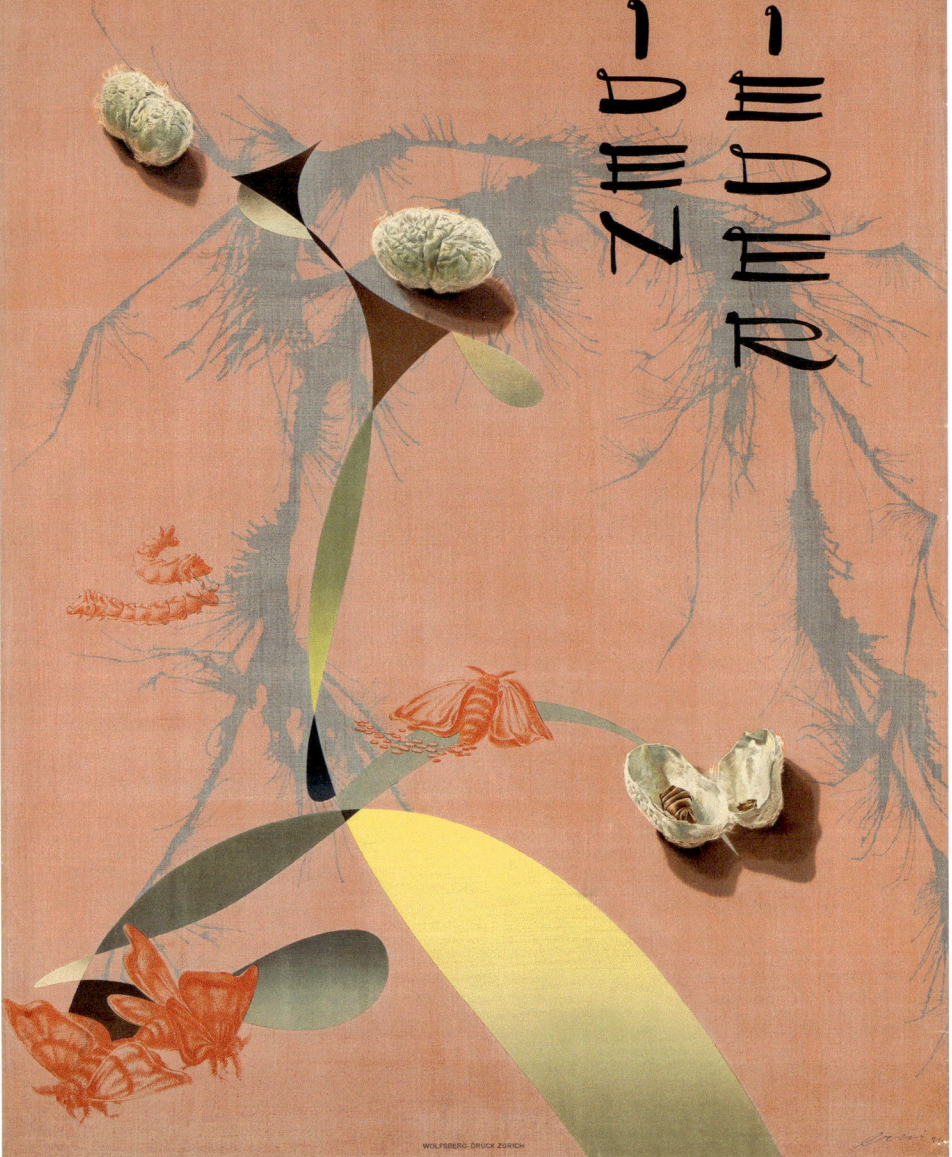

7 **Hans Erni**
Seiden Grieder
1946

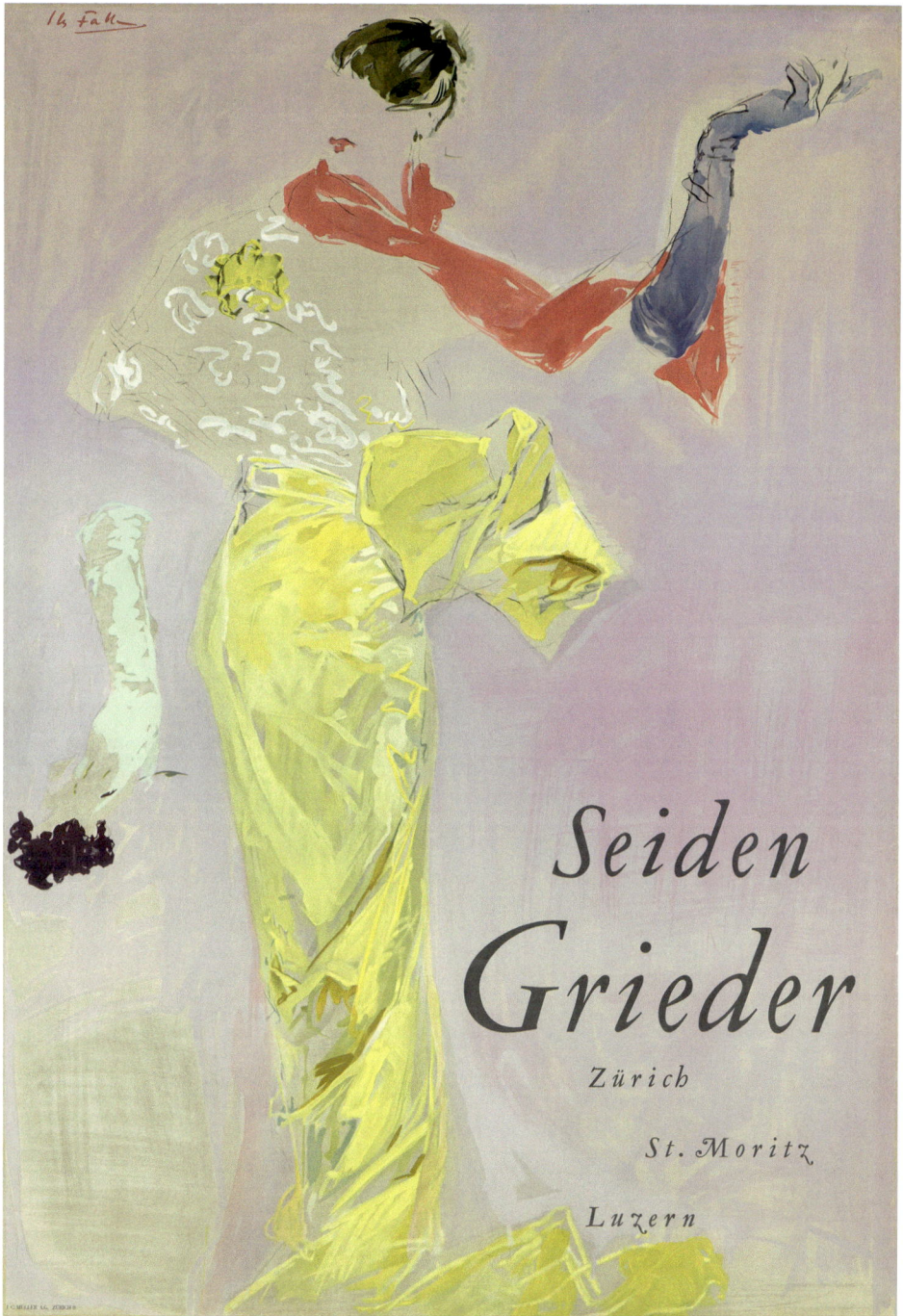

8 **Hans Falk**
Seiden Grieder
1950

9 **Charles Honoré Loupot**
Seiden-Grieder
1918

10 **Hans Falk**
PKZ
1944

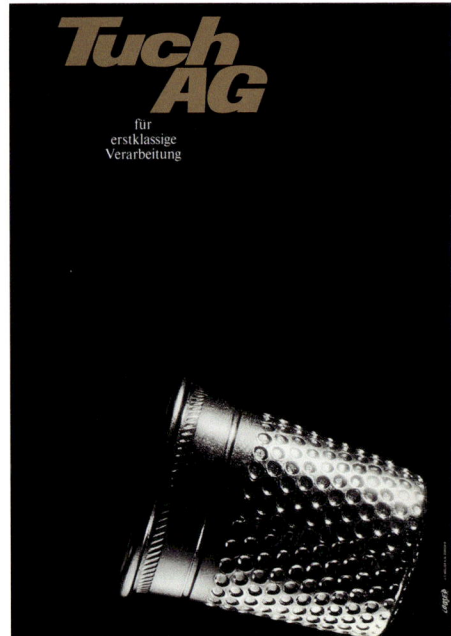

11 **Peter Birkhäuser**
PKZ
1934

12 **Wirz Werbung / Sandro Bocola**
Die besten Stoffe der Welt verarbeitet PKZ
1961

13 **Wirz Werbung / Sandro Bocola**
Handarbeit hat hohe Geltung bei PKZ
1961

14 **Hans Looser**
Tuch AG für erstklassige Verarbeitung
1961

15 **Otto Baumberger**
Marque PKZ
1923

16 **Stephan Krotowski**
Marke PKZ / Burger-Kehl & Co
1913

17 **Otto Morach**
Jedermann PKZ
1928

18 **Ludwig Hohlwein**
Marque PKZ
1908

19 **Herbert Matter**
PKZ
1928

20 **Viktor Rutz** (zugeschrieben / ascribed to)
Pelz Kuhn
ca. 1932

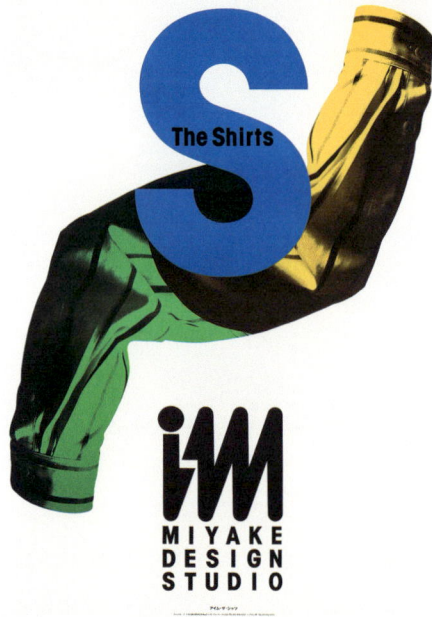

21 **Masaaki Hiromura, Takafumi Kusagaya**
Miyake Design Studio / Necktie
1990

22 **Masaaki Hiromura, Takafumi Kusagaya**
Miyake Design Studio / Jackets
1990

23 **Masaaki Hiromura, Takafumi Kusagaya**
Miyake Design Studio / The Shirts
1990

24 **Heini Fischer**
PKZ
1952

25 **Otto Baumberger**
PKZ zieht um
1925

26 **Joseph Binder**
Der Jawo Mantel
1930

27 **Atelier Eidenbenz / Hanspeter Rolly**
Tuch AG
1957

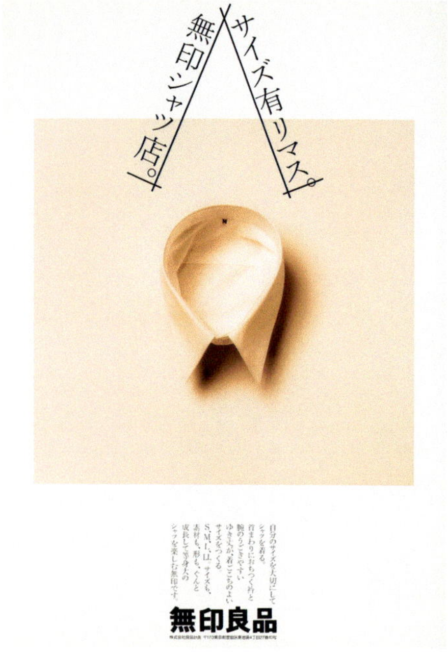

28 **Masaaki Hiromura, Toshiyuki Kojima**
Muji Shirt Store / Various Sizes Available
1990

29 **Atelier Eidenbenz**
Tuch AG
1948

30 **Elso Schiavo**
Mode Zehnder
1972

31 **Peter Birkhäuser**
Durable
1951

32 **K. D. Geissbühler**
Dschingis
1978

33 **Roman Cieślewicz**
Moda Polska Warszawa
1959

34 **Salvatore Gregorietti**
IR / Estate indiana
1968

"Spiel mit Stil"

GRIEDER
LES BOUTIQUES

35 **Transphère**
Grieder Les Boutiques
1997

"Jeux d'élégances"

36 **Transphère**
Bon Génie Les Boutiques
1996

37 **Rogivue & Schmid**
Barbados Jeans
1972

38 **Max Linder Werbeagentur / Peter Christian Jost**
Lee Cooper
1971

39 **Amrein-Pieren**
Ciolina / La Mode
1994

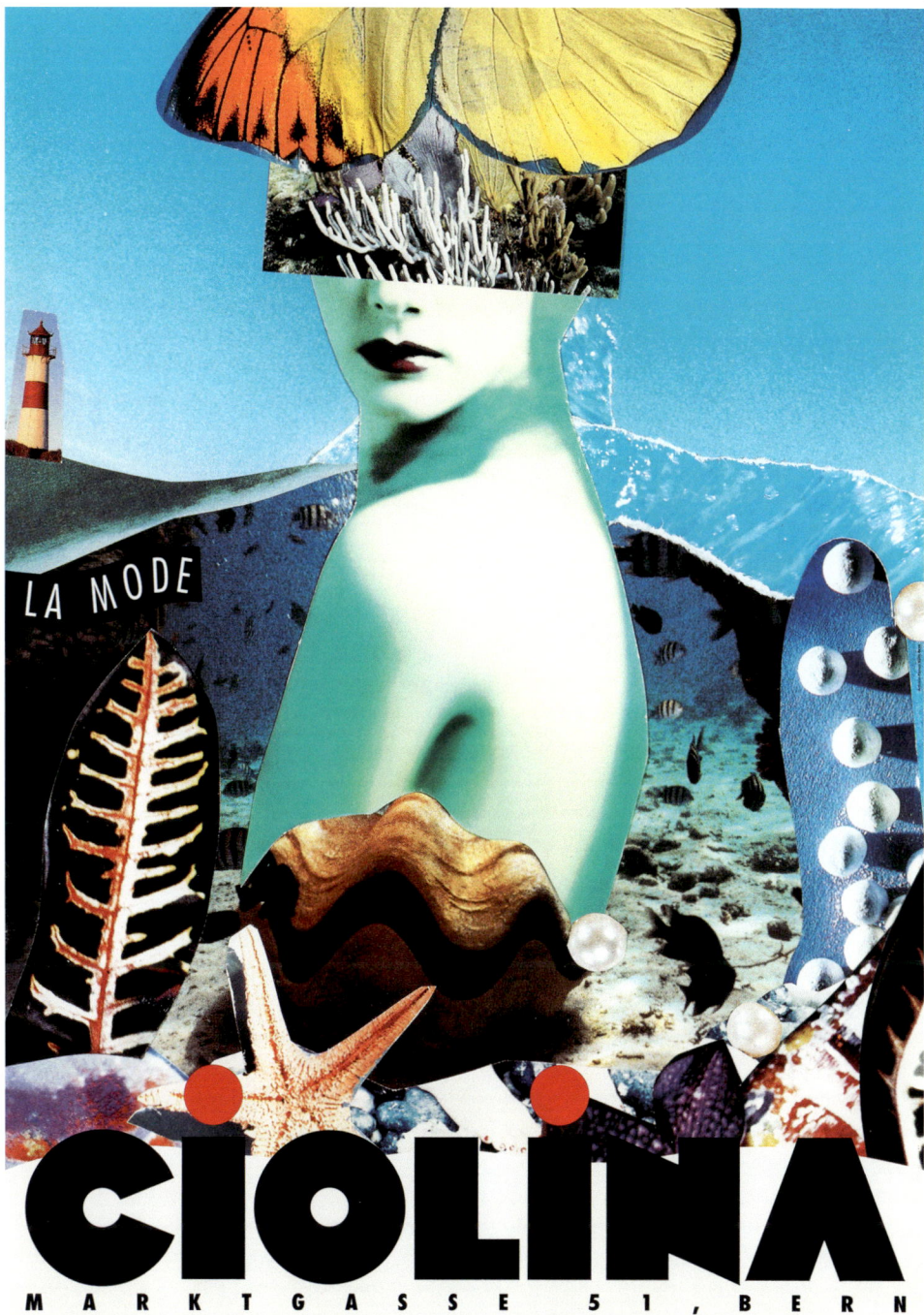

40 **Amrein-Pieren**
Ciolina / La Mode
1994

READING FASHION MOODS: A VISUAL HISTORY OF FASHION

Elke Gaugele

Fashion is a system that translates clothing into the "language of fashion" within the frame of the media.[1] Since the onset of modernity, the production of clothing as fashion has played a key role, mediated by images, the media, advertising, and posters, which are presented here as a visual history of fashion spanning over a hundred years. Fashion media shape time and space and, by transforming them, render contemporaneity aesthetically tangible. As a paradigm for culture, progress, and innovation, fashion defined superiority and the look of the "civilized" West in modernity's colonial power structure. This includes cultural appropriation processes and the aesthetic incorporation of an exotic "Other" that is illustrated by the Orientalist Art Nouveau poster 1 at the start of this publication. To this day, fashion continues to give form, via the body, to "the passage from sentience to meaning,"[2] communicating models, values, and norms of identity, ethnicity, gender, class, and nation. In an era of digital fashion media, booming African fashion cities, and Modest Fashion Weeks in Dubai, Jakarta, and London, fashion is influencing global hierarchies and economies–along with individuality and community.

CLOTHING AND FASHION

As reflected in early posters, clothes and fashion represent different concepts and economies, particularly with respect to added and material value. Thorstein Veblen's comments at the turn of the century on "dress as an expression of the pecuniary culture" referenced how clothes derive their commercial value by promising consumers beauty and alluring added value.[3] Yet well into the postwar period, posters still emphatically showed that their main focus was on clothes and dressing. While department stores launched mass production of suits and off-the-peg garments in standardized sizes, the posters insisted that clothes should not shift status to become primarily fashion. Slogans like "the world's best fabrics" (PKZ) 12, "first-rate workmanship" (Tuch AG) 14, and "durable" 31 emphasize the garments' "good design," lasting quality, craftsmanship, and thus material value. The posters' distance to and neutral stance on fashion testify to subtle differences and a distinction that seeks to view class, style, and perhaps the whole nation in terms of simplicity, objectivity, and masculinity. Elegant men (in groups) wearing dark, striped, or checked suits, long coats, and hats 16–18 illustrate the uniform of modern masculinity. Poster designers thus establish aesthetic links between suits, coats, and uniforms, between business and the military. Until the postwar era, the posters barely reflected modern fashion as a haute couture product or as a contemporary phenomenon of representative femininity, assigned to and worn by women. The rare female figures represent luxury as an exotic animalistic "Other": expressionistically theatrical in furs 20 or in Zurich firm Seiden-Grieder's voluminous wrap robe, inspired by couturier Paul Poiret 9. Women only began to appear in fashion posters more frequently in the 1950s–for example, in the advertisements

1 Roland Barthes [1967], *The Fashion System,* New York 1985.
2 Ibid., p. 258.
3 Thorstein Veblen [1899], "Dress as an Expression of the Pecuniary Culture," in: *The Theory of the Leisure Class: An Economic Study of Institutions,* New York 1912, pp. 167–187.

created by Max Huber and Lora Lamm for Milan's innovative department store La Rinascente. The language of fashion for industrially manufactured clothing 44 accompanied them, defining their spheres of action: "La Moda 1960–per la città, i viaggi, la professione" 43.

FROM ARTISANSHIP TO GLOBAL FACTORY

"PKZ values excellent needlework"–this was the motto accompanying a 1961 photo of the director of the firm, sitting cross-legged with needle and thread 13. In a white shirt and tie, peering intently through his glasses, the "boss" himself sews in the shiny lining by hand. When designer Sandro Bocola and photographer Max Emil Buchmann staged this scene, over 1,000 seamstresses and mostly female staff were working for PKZ in two factories in Zurich and Massagno and at fifteen branches in all major Swiss cities; however, the poster evokes a gesture of contemplative calm in the emerging fast-paced era of globalization. Just five years later, the firm encountered its first problems. Rising rents, capital costs, and customs barriers meant its Swiss textile manufacturing was discontinued in 1974 and production was outsourced abroad. Today it is handled in China, India, and (southeastern) Europe. In 1978, Switzerland's first H&M store exemplified the turn to fast fashion. From 1989 on, over fifteen European countries reacted to outsourcing of textile production to low-wage countries, free trade zones, and sweatshops–with long hours, low pay, and unhealthy workplaces–by launching national fair fashion campaigns. These represent a protest by civil society against fashion's new equation: the shift to image instead of quality. The growing role of images and logos for corporate revenue led to soaring advertising budgets for stars and super-models, who characterize the branding era with its accelerated cycles of low-wage fashion production. Moving into the digital age, competition for consumer attention means larger billboards along with more intense visual campaigns, turning the body into fashion with a flood of perfect physiques. The posters reflect the rise of large mul-tinational brands since the 1980s, their logos sprawled across human torsos and public space, from luxury brands to jeans and high street brands 101–104, 111–130.

FASHION AND ETHICS

"Empty your closets" and "I want my clothes back"–in 1993, the Benetton Group pro-moted a clothing redistribution project with images of a naked Luciano Benetton cov-ered by large black letters: consumers were called on to donate second-hand clothing to Swiss Caritas, the Red Cross, and the Red Crescent 115. With this marketing cam-paign, Oliviero Toscani, who worked for Benetton from 1982 to 2000 and from 2017 to 2020, aimed to refute accusations directed at his previous "shock campaigns" that he exploited others' tragedies to promote the brand's global expansion and profits 4. In 1992, Toscani began to appropriate topical press photos for Benetton ads in the tradition of concerned photography,[4] which adopts a humanitarian tone and views photography as a medium to change the world.[5] Instead of hiring supermodels or celebrities, he created socio-critical advertising posters on societal issues like racism,

4 Cornell Capa (ed.), *The Concerned Photographer: The Photographs of Werner Bischof, André Kertész, Robert Capa, Leonard Freed, David Seymour ("Chim"), Dan Weiner,* New York 1968.
5 See Bettina Richter, "Contemporary 'Iconoclasts,'" in: Museum für Gestaltung Zürich, Bettina Richter (eds.), *Help!, Poster Collection 20,* Baden 2009, p. 70/71.

disability, homosexuality, AIDS, or the death penalty. Ever since, a highly regarded spectrum of globalization-critical documentary photos, condemning abuses and even sparking controversy in court, has circulated under the company's logo. Intermeshed with the group's neoliberal globalization strategies, this visual and image production reflects the contradiction that Luc Boltanski and Ève Chiapello dub the "new spirit of capitalism": "How can participation in capitalist firms be justified in terms of the common good and how, confronted with accusations of injustice, can the way it is conducted and managed be defended?"[6] However, this paradox characterizes fashion's entire development in the Anthropocene and helped trigger the ethical turn in twenty-first-century fashion, which led a growing number of designers, such as Vivienne Westwood, Bruno Pieters, Christopher Raeburn, and Stella McCartney, to adopt environmental activist stances. This development is also documented by the Diesel campaigns "Nature–Love It While It Lasts" (2004) 75 and "Global Warming Ready" (2007) 125, as well as by Levi's campaigns (2008) 99, 100. With the "United Victims of Benetton" poster, activists demanded compensation for victims and survivors of the Rana Plaza disaster in Bangladesh, which in April 2013 claimed the lives of over 1,100 workers and injured thousands more. The Benetton Group, which, like Primark, Lee Cooper, Zara, and Mango, had purchased textiles from Rana Plaza, did not sign the UN Global Compact until 2015, when it (voluntarily) committed to respect human and labor rights and protect the environment.

ART AS A LANGUAGE OF FASHION
Conceptual approaches to fashion have existed since the early twentieth century. Elsa Schiaparelli's iconic shoe hat, for example, inspired a Polish fashion poster in the late 1950s 33. Surrealist motifs, wordmarks, and Dadaist collage permeate twentieth-century fashion posters. Although modernist theory positions fashion and art on distinct time axes, with Charles Baudelaire regarding art as "eternal and immutable"[7] and fashion as "the ephemeral, the fleeting, the coincidental,"[8] postmodernism brings their dynamics ever closer together.

Since the 1970s, Issey Miyake 81–84, Yōhji Yamamoto, and Rei Kawakubo–the "Japanese Fashion Revolution" avant-garde–have cooperated with artists and museums in developing, marketing, and producing images for their collections. Minimalist presentations in White Cube stores of their monochrome, sculptural, asymmetrical looks, which are loose-fit and often appear unfinished or worn, challenged beauty conventions and wearing habits. 1980s Parisian fashion shows by Japanese-influenced Martin Margiela and the Antwerp Six also contributed significantly to the emergence of a new era of conceptual fashion. Since the mid-1990s, a new generation of designers has been working on conceptual approaches to deconstructing and reconstructing fashion system aesthetics. Initially an avant-garde countermovement to the fashion industry with the motto "Not in Fashion!" they have since recalibrated how fashion relates to art or to anti-fashion, and how design relates to fashion criticism. At the same time,

6 Luc Boltanski and Ève Chiapello [1999], *The New Spirit of Capitalism,* London 2005, p. 16.
7 Charles Baudelaire [1860], "The Painter of Modern Life," in: Jonathan Mayne (ed. and transl.), *The Painter of Modern Life and Other Essays,* London 1964, p. 13.
8 Ibid., p. 13.

a veritable co-branding of the fashion and art system began, as luxury brands increasingly cooperated with artists or sponsored exhibitions and biennials. As designers increasingly showed work in contemporary art contexts and brands like Prada opened museums to house their art collections, fashion also became a principle informing form and content for many artists, such as Dutch photographers Inez van Lamsweerde and Vinoodh Matadin. Together with art and design duo M/M (Paris), they produced *The Alphabet* in 2001, an "A to Z of beauty" 65–68, in which cut-outs of models' photographs formed a "female" typography. In 1990, Masaaki Hiromura had spelled out the language of fashion with art's letters for Issey Miyake 21–23.

VISUAL POP

The Japanese posters read like a mood board for Tokyo's rapid rise as the epicenter of fashion and street style. They formed the visual soundtrack for the 1980s transition from New Wave to Japan's first avant-garde fashion trend, dubbed the "designer and character" boom. Makoto Saito was part of the scene and made no-slogan posters that drew on American pop aesthetics, working for labels such as Ba-Tsu, Alpha Cubic, Jun Men, and Kind Wear 85–98. Japanese fast-fashion brands, like teenager lingerie label Une nana cool 74, picked up on this trend too. New large shopping centers hothoused the art, fashion, and pop culture crossover, as pioneers of Japanese "fashion building" and youth culture trendsetters. Laforet Harajuku 62, 64, 72, known by locals as the "fashion panopticon," opened in 1978 with around 150 stores and a museum. Shibuya Parco 73 has run its own trend-watching agency for street-fashion marketing since 1977. In the 1990s, Vivre commissioned Masami Shimizu 58, 61, 63 and Jun Shibata 57 to create posters in a conceptual art style, and in the 2000s, it turned to pop artist Nagi Noda 71 for a flamboyant fitness poster that drew parallels between female and poodle body styling, with ironic allusions inter alia to Jeff Koons. By contrast, designer Rikako Nagashima visualized higher spheres for Dictionary in "Mind of Telepathy" 5.

Youth cultures have developed globally as visual popscapes, from images of hippies in a state of enlightenment to commodification of punk or Kawaiian style, normcore, and Instagram poses. Ads for boutiques and labels in the 1970s and 1980s Swiss fashion boom also drew on pop culture collage and silkscreen aesthetics: Punch 107, Dschingis 32, Thema Selection, Drake Store 106, Löw Boutique 47–50 or Au père et fils 108. Jeans became a vector for the global language of youth culture rebellion, with images of bodies, gender, and desire. As Erving Goffman explains in *Gender Advertisements*, these are structured by hierarchies and submission rituals.[9] The 1970s revolved around heterosexual couples' yearning for nature–in a boat on a lonely beach 37 or as Tarzan and Jane in the jungle 109–negotiating the topos of freedom through naked torsos 38. Fashions shape sexuality through unisex jeans or hyper-realistic sexist images of "dream jeans" 101. Moving into the twenty-first century, fashion has produced a wide range of queer LGBTQ+ identities, anticipated by the muscular cowboy, as a proxy for the gay community 130.

9 Erving Goffman, *Gender Advertisements,* Washington 1976.

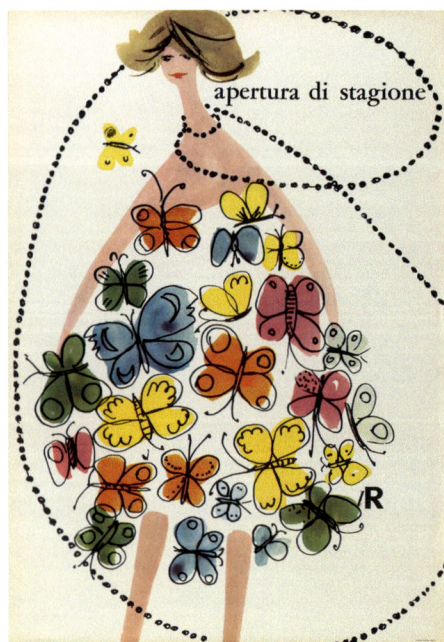

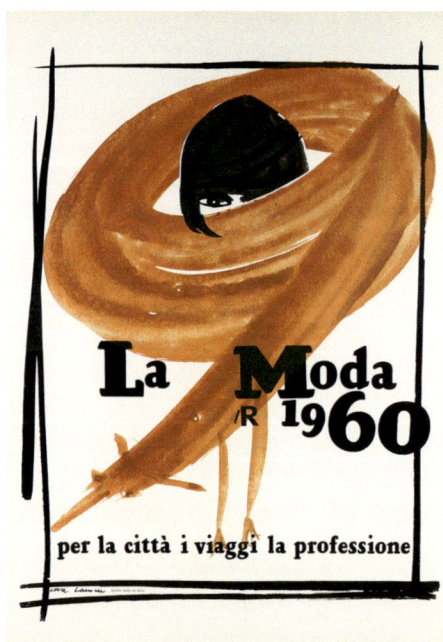

41 **Lora Lamm**
La Rinascente / Estate e moda
1958

43 **Lora Lamm**
IR / La moda 1960
1960

42 **Lora Lamm**
IR / Apertura di stagione
1957

LA MODA ATTUALE È LA CONFEZIONE

LA
CONFECTION
RÉGIT
LA MODE
ACTUELLE

TODAY'S
FASHION
IS
CONFECTION

44 **Lora Lamm**
La moda attuale è la confezione
1959

45 **Max Huber**
Per voi tutta la moda / È l'autunno della Rinascente
1954

46 **Max Huber**
La Rinascente / Moda autunno–inverno 1955
1955

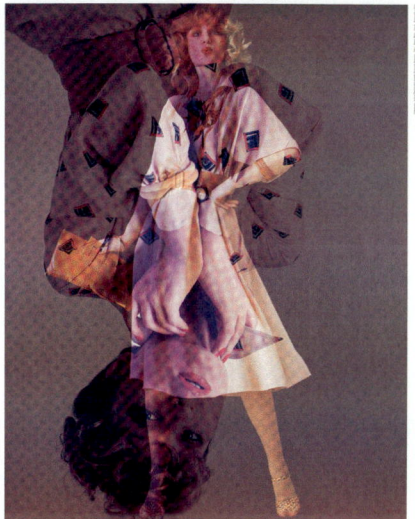

47–50 **Atelier Hablützel und Jaquet /
Reinhart Morscher**
Löw Boutique
1975

51 **Christian Coigny**
Grieder
1978

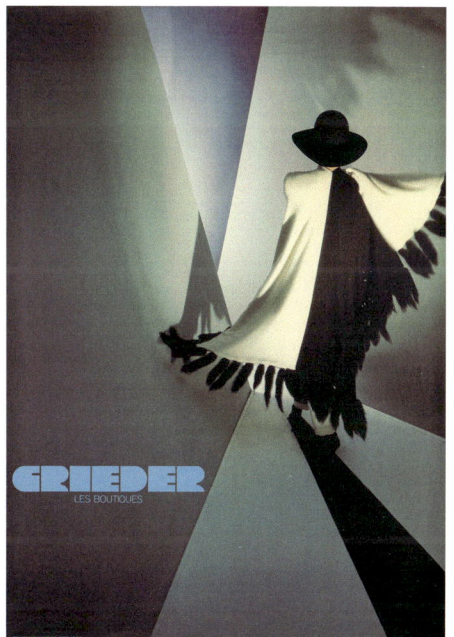

52 **Christian Coigny**
Grieder
1982

53 **Christian Coigny**
Grieder
1977

54 **Christian Coigny**
Grieder
1979

55 **Christian Coigny**
Grieder Les Boutiques
ca. 1983

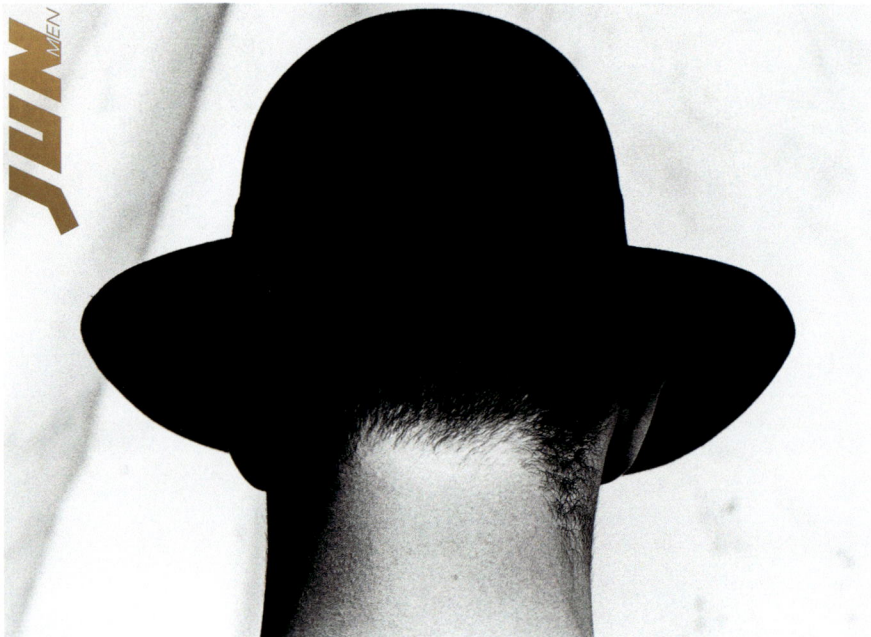

56 **Makoto Saito**
Jun Men
1986

57 **Jun Shibata**
Vivre
1992

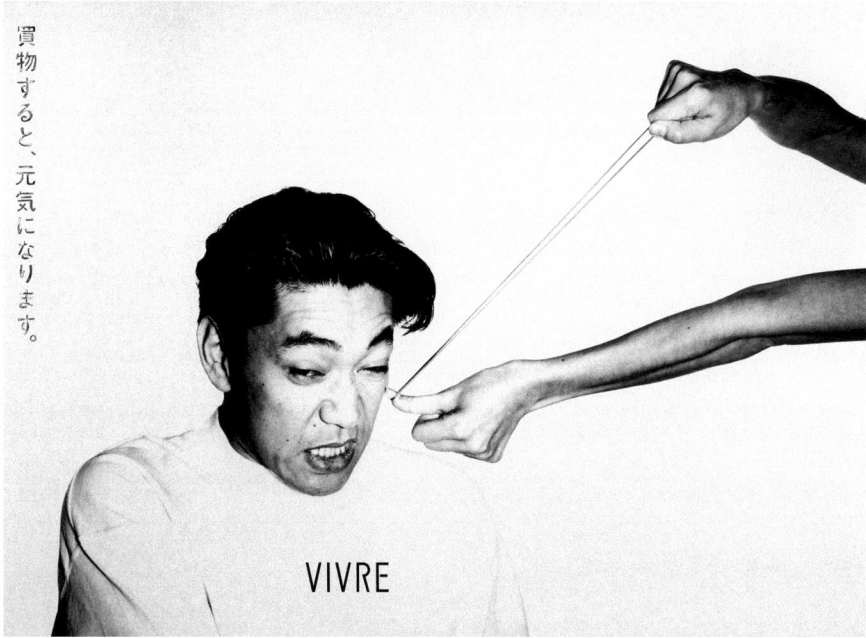

58 **Masami Shimizu**
Vivre, 1992

59/60 **Rhyner & Haettenschweiler / Thomas Rhyner,
Sasha Haettenschweiler**
Pink Flamingo
1991

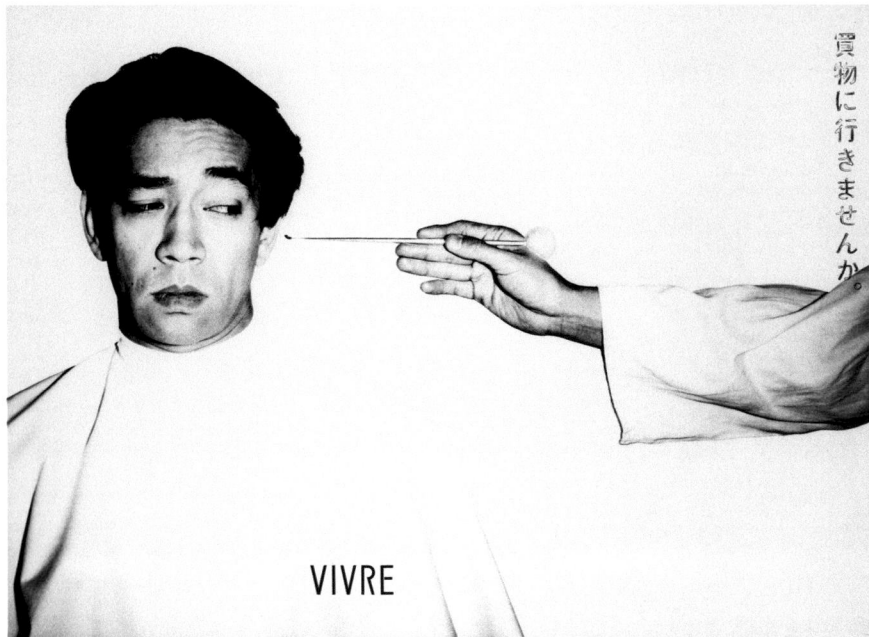

61 **Masami Shimizu**
Vivre
1992

62 **Takuya Onuki, Yuichi Shimabayashi**
Laforet
1991

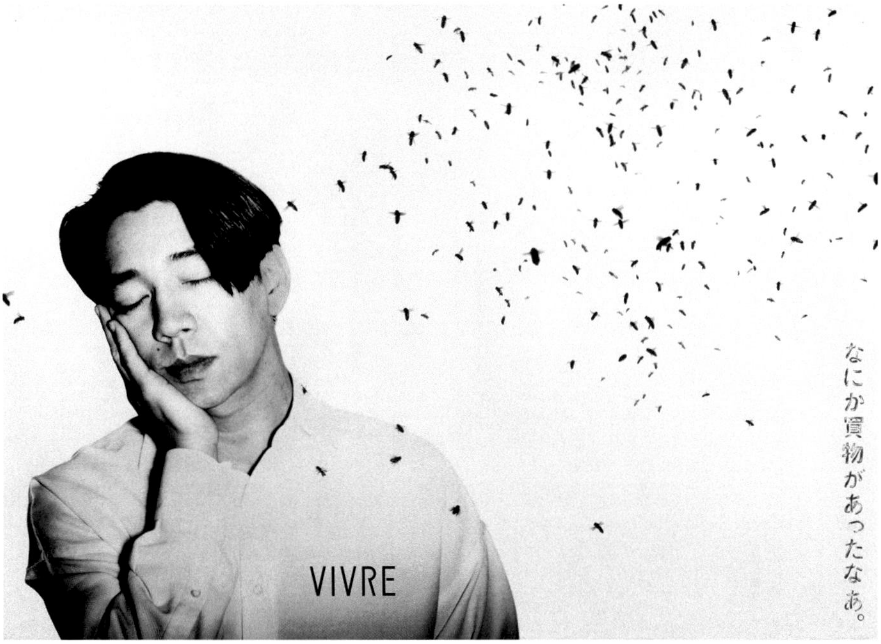

なにか買物があったなぁ。

VIVRE

63 **Masami Shimizu**
Vivre
1992

64 **Takuya Onuki, Yuichi Shimabayashi**
Laforet
1991

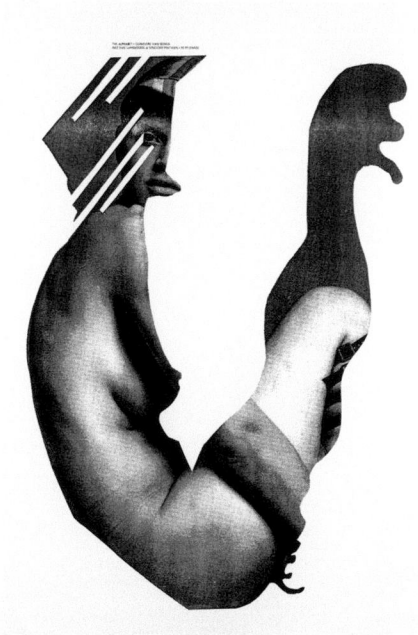

65 **M/M (Paris) / Michael Amzalag,**
Mathias Augustyniak
S / The Alphabet, 2001

66 **M/M (Paris) / Michael Amzalag,**
Mathias Augustyniak
W / The Alphabet, 2001

67 **M/M (Paris) / Michael Amzalag,**
Mathias Augustyniak
V / The Alphabet, 2001

68 **M/M (Paris) / Michael Amzalag,**
Mathias Augustyniak
X / The Alphabet, 2001

69/70 **Makoto Saito**
1986 Alpha Cubic
1986

71 **Nagi Noda**
Vivre
2004

LAFORET HAPPY ANNIVERSARY

72 **Nagi Noda**
Laforet
2005

73 **Tomoko Ikeda, Hiromi Oji, Masami Shimizu**
Parco
1989

74 **Draft Co.**
Une nana cool
2003

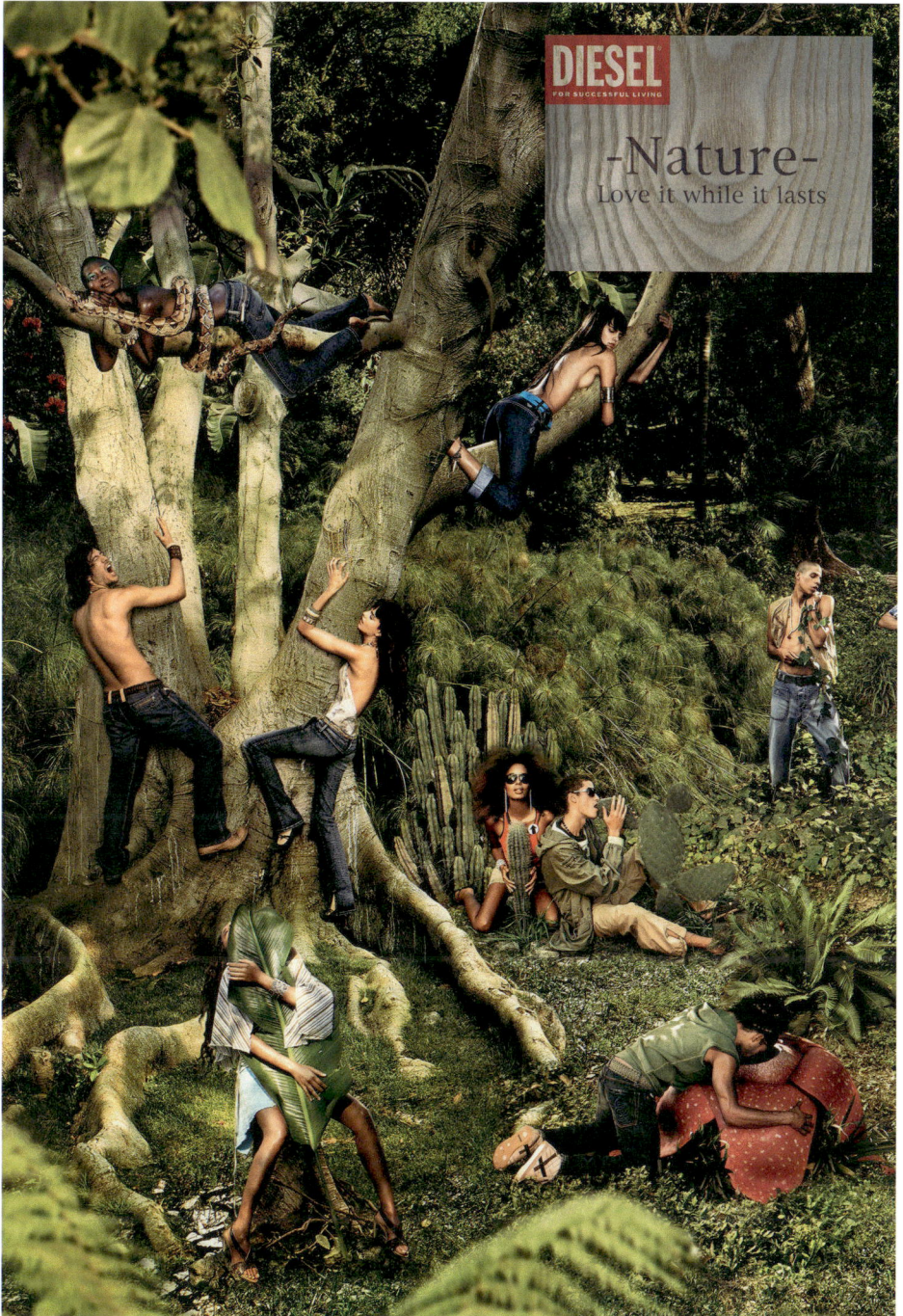

75 **Anonym**
Diesel / Nature
2004

76 **Makoto Saito**
Onward
1995

長

組曲

The global staff of Onward presents a highly sensitive international brand for contemporary fashion-loving women.

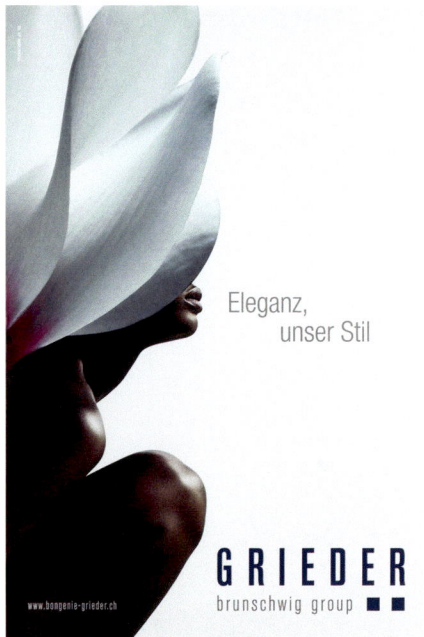

Eleganz,
unser Stil

GRIEDER
brunschwig group ■ ■

www.bongenie-grieder.ch

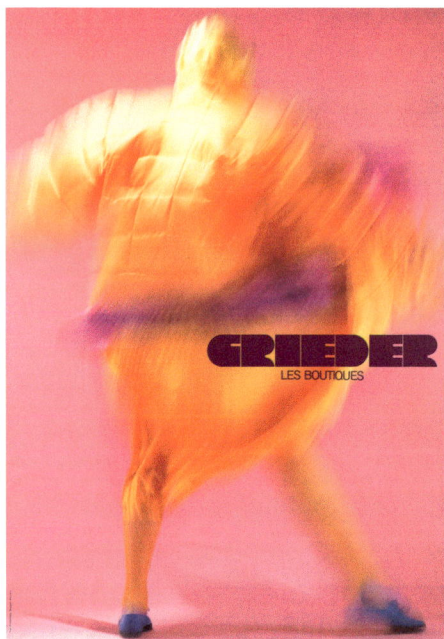

77 **Christian Coigny, Werner Jeker**
Grieder Les Boutiques
1986

78 **Christian Coigny**
Grieder Les Boutiques
1984

79 **Transphère**
Grieder Brunschwig Group
2008

80 **Christian Coigny**
Grieder Les Boutiques
1985

81 **Ikko Tanaka**
Issey Miyake 1999
1999

82 **Ikko Tanaka**
Issey Miyake 1999
1999

83 **Ikko Tanaka**
Issey Miyake 1998
1998

84 **Ikko Tanaka**
Issey Miyake / Making Things
2000

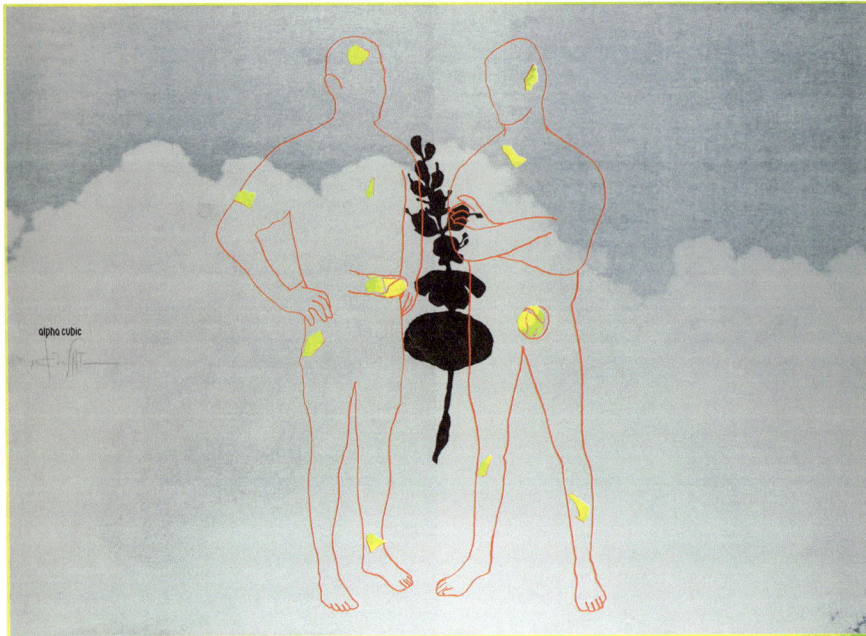

85/86 **Makoto Saito**
Alpha Cubic
1990

GEFÜHLSSACHE –
MODEPLAKATE VON MAKOTO SAITO
Bettina Richter

«Dadurch, dass man etwas ungesagt lässt, gibt man dem Betrachter die Möglichkeit, die Idee zu vollenden. Damit fesselt ein grosses Meisterwerk die Aufmerksamkeit so unwiderstehlich, bis du selber ein Teil davon zu werden scheinst. Ein Vakuum ist da, in das du hineingehen und das du mit deinem ästhetischen Gefühl bis an den Rand füllen musst.»[1]

Das Zitat des japanischen Kulturphilosophen Kakuzō Okakura ist charakteristisch für das Schönheitsempfinden seines Landes und lässt sich selbst auf moderne Kommunikationsmittel übertragen. Das hochästhetische japanische Plakat hängt in öffentlich zugänglichen Innenräumen – U-Bahn-Stationen, Kaufhäusern und so weiter –, möchte ebendort als Kunstwerk wirken und intime Momente der Ruhe und visuellen Entspannung anbieten. Makoto Saitos Arbeiten führen beispielhaft vor Augen, dass Poesie und Andeutung, die Abstrahierung konkreter Motive auch in der Fashionwerbung funktionieren. Seine Plakate für die Modehäuser Ba-Tsu oder Alpha Cubic verweigern sich jeder eindeutigen Lesart und verzichten auf eine klare Werbebotschaft. Hingegen entwerfen sie eine Unternehmensidentität, die sich durch die Wahl der künstlerischen Position Saitos auszeichnet. Jeder Versuch einer illusionistischen Wiedergabe der Dinge gilt in der japanischen Kultur als geist- und fantasieloser Betrug. Saitos experimentelles Spiel mit Verfremdungseffekten durch Pars pro toto, Cut-up-Bilder oder angeschnittene Motive, durch Überlagerungen und malerische Gesten ermöglicht Freiraum für die individuelle Interpretation und verführt das Publikum emotional. Sein souveräner Umgang mit Leerraum und das spannungsvolle Zusammenwirken von Grund und Motiv verleihen den Dingen eine ungewöhnliche Suggestionskraft. Körperfragmente im White Cube, vielfach gebrochene, mehrperspektivische Gesichter oder für visuelle Geschichten aufgespannte Bühnenräume vermitteln ein Lebensgefühl von heftiger Intensität. Die Unvollkommenheit mancher Plakate verstärkt diese Wahrnehmung noch: Saitos Misstrauen gegenüber jeder computergenerierten Perfektion führt zu einem Gestaltungsprozess, in dem die Maschine höchstens als finales Werkzeug dient. Saito möchte erklärtermassen den Akt des Sehens hinterfragen, die Erwartungen des Publikums irritieren und zugleich übertreffen. Der Erfolg seiner Plakate beruht paradoxerweise auf der bewussten Verletzung aller vermeintlichen Regeln der Plakatgestaltung. Saitos Plakate widersetzen sich aber auch einer Vermarktungslogik, die das Produkt zentral platziert. Das Essenzielle jeder PR-Strategie, sowohl im Osten als auch im Westen, hat Saito jedoch meisterhaft begriffen: Gelungene visuelle Kommunikation spricht ihre Kundschaft in erster Linie auf der Gefühlsebene an.

«La raison a toujours raison kann keine Gültigkeit haben, denn Design in Japan ist Gefühlssache, keine Sache der Logik, der intelligenten Raumaufteilung von Fläche, Bild und Schrift.»[2]

A QUESTION OF FEELING–
FASHION POSTERS BY MAKOTO SAITO
Bettina Richter

"In leaving something unsaid, the beholder is given the chance to complete the idea and thus a great masterpiece irresistibly rivets your attention until you seem to become actually a part of it. A vacuum is there for you to enter and to fill up to the full measure of your aesthetic emotion."[1]

This quotation from Kakuzō Okakura, a Japanese cultural philosophy scholar, exemplifies his country's sense of beauty and even applies to modern means of communication. Highly aesthetic Japanese posters in interiors with public access–subway stations, department stores, and so on–are intended to function as artworks in this context, offering intimate moments of peace and visual relaxation. Makoto Saito's works epitomize how poetry, evocation, and abstractions of concrete motifs also function in fashion advertising. His posters for the brands Ba-Tsu or Alpha Cubic evade unambiguous readings and dispense with a clear-cut promotional message. Instead, they define a corporate identity informed by the choice of Saito's artistic position. Attempted illusionistic renderings are considered vacuous, unimaginative frauds in Japanese culture. Saito's playful experiments with defamiliarization effects–achieved through a pars pro toto technique, cut-up images, cropped motifs, superpositions, and painterly gestures–offer leeway for individual interpretation and seduce the audience emotionally. His self-assured handling of empty space and the tense interplay between ground and motif imbue the objects with unusual evocative force. Fragmented bodies in a White Cube, a plethora of fractured, multi-perspective faces, or stages that are configured for visual storytelling convey an extremely intense attitude. The imperfection of certain posters reinforces this perception: Saito's distrust of flawless computer-generated images leads to a design process that incorporates this mechanical aspect, if at all, only right at the end. His stated aim is to question the act of vision, confounding and simultaneously surpassing audience expectations. Paradoxically, his posters' success stems from deliberately breaking all purported rules of poster design while defying a marketing logic that sets the product center stage. Saito has nonetheless mastered the essence of all PR strategies, in the East or the West: successful visual communication appeals primarily to customers' emotions.

"La raison a toujours raison will not do here, for design in Japan is a matter of feeling, not of logic, of the intelligent spatial apportioning of surface, image and script."[2]

1 Kakuzō Okakura [1906], *Das Buch vom Tee,* Frankfurt a. M. / Leipzig 1989, S. 48.
2 Helmut Schmid, *Japan japanisch – die leise Schönheit japanischer Dinge,* Tokio 2012, S. 24.

1 Kakuzō Okakura [1906], *The Book of Tea,* Edinburgh / London 1919, p. 61.
2 Helmut Schmid, *Japan Japanese–The Quiet Beauty of Things Japanese,* Tokyo 2012, p. 24.

Design by Makoto Saito   Produce by Rioji Matsumoto

87 **Makoto Saito**
Ba-Tsu 1994
1994

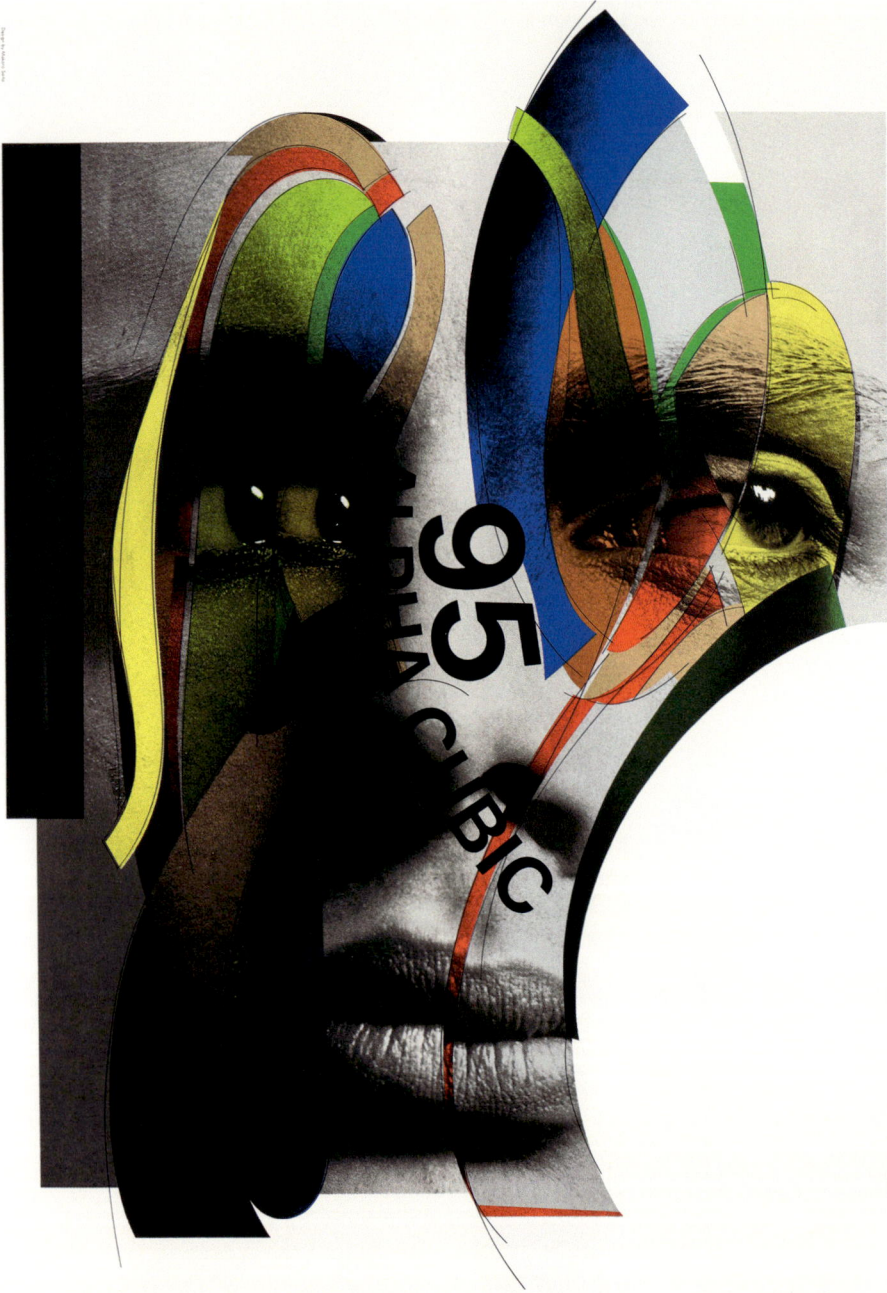

88 **Makoto Saito**
Alpha Cubic 95
1995

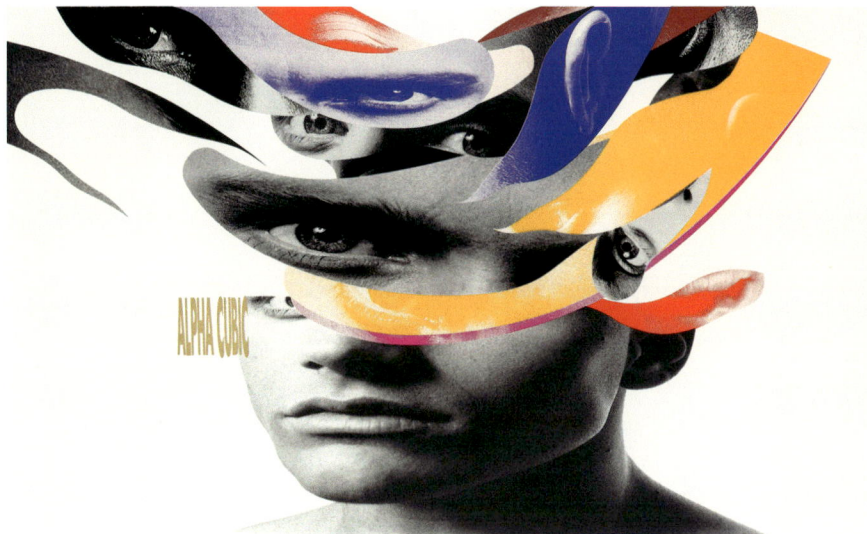

89 **Makoto Saito, Eiichiro Sakata**
Alpha Cubic
1988

90 **Makoto Saito**
Alpha Cubic 1987
1987

91 **Makoto Saito**
Kind Wear
1989

92 **Makoto Saito**
Kind Wear
1989

93 **Makoto Saito**
0001 Alpha Cubic
1988

94 **Makoto Saito**
1992 / Kind Wear
1992

Bulbs.

Tubers.

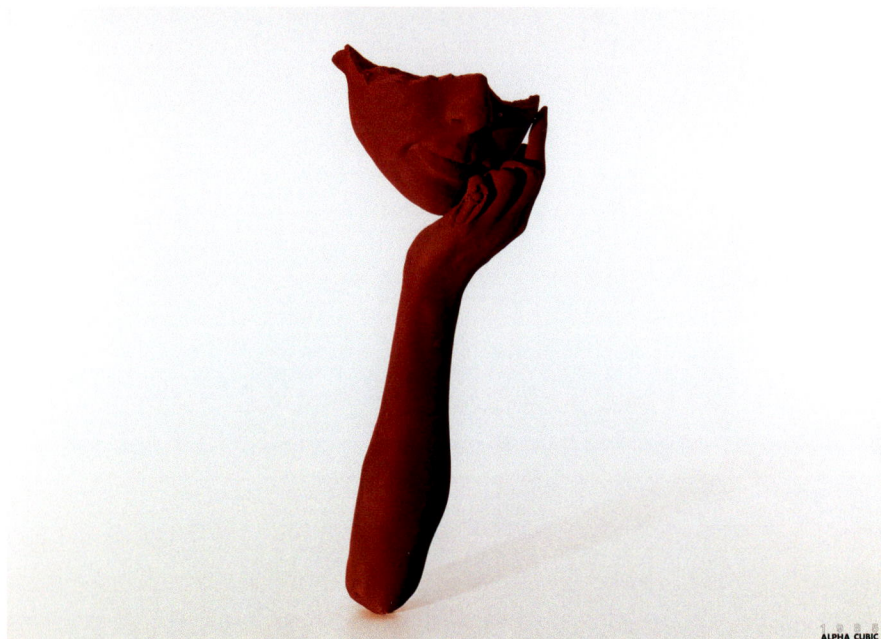

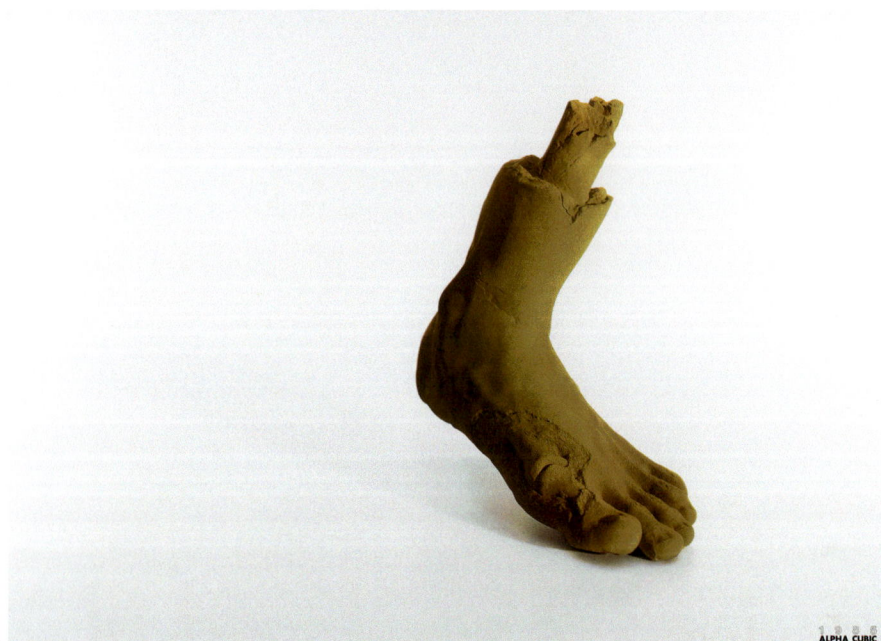

95/96 **Makoto Saito**
1985 Alpha Cubic
1985

97 **Makoto Saito**
Alpha Cubic for Joseph Beuys
1984

98 **Makoto Saito**
Kind Wear
1988

99 **Sagmeister / Joe Shouldice, Richard The**
This Is a Pair of Levi's
2008

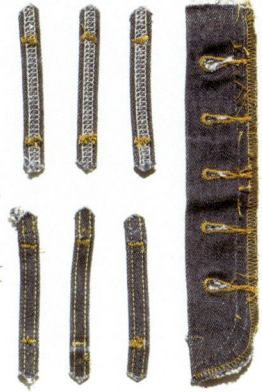

100 **Sagmeister / Joe Shouldice, Richard The**
[ohne Text – no text]
2008

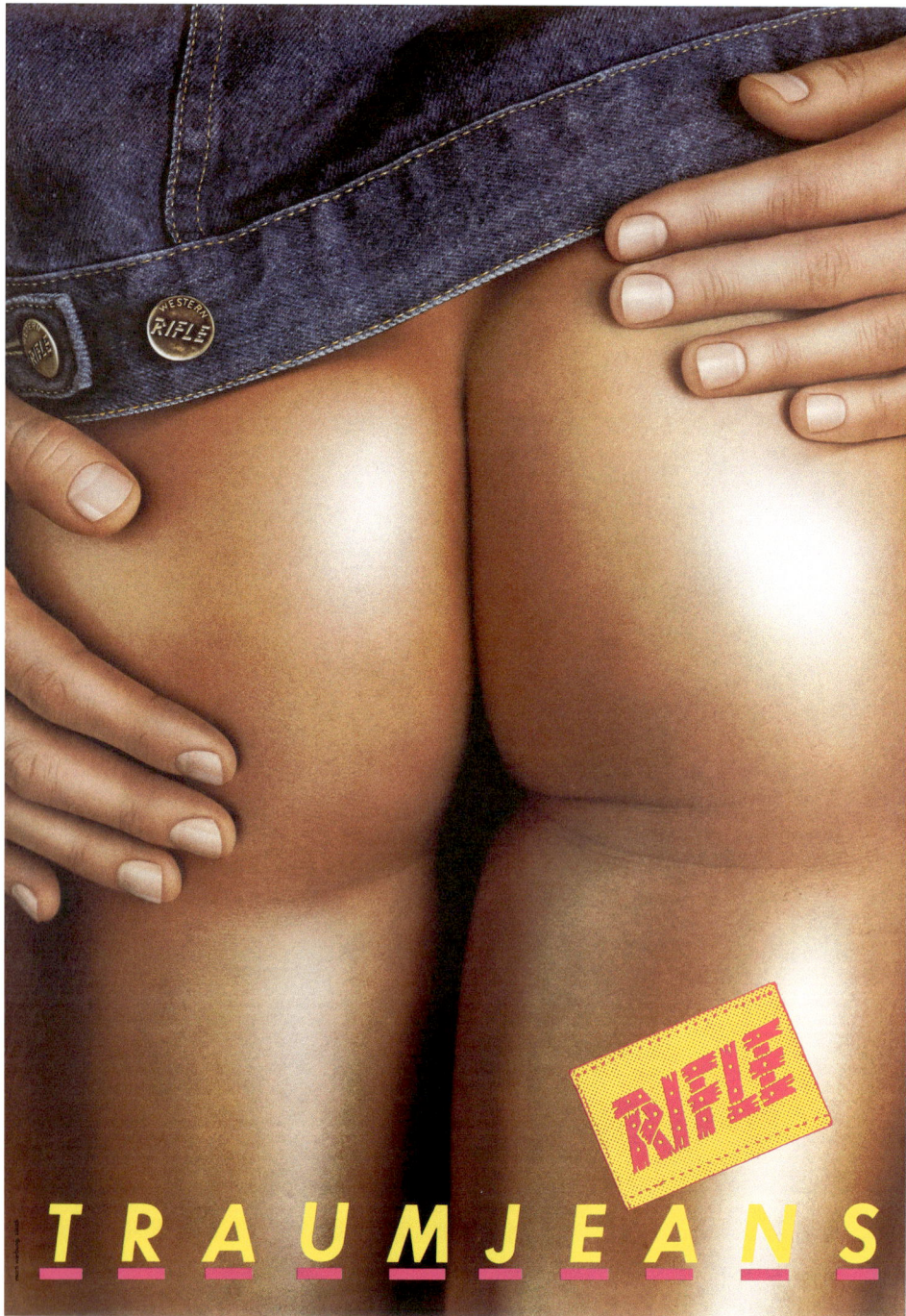

101 **Peter Marti**
Rifle Traumjeans
1982

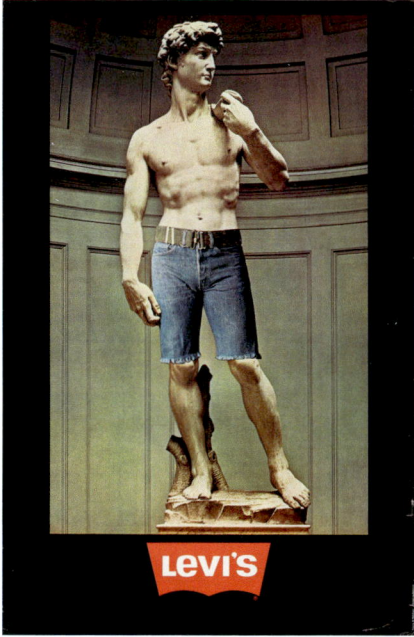

102 **Advico-Delpire**
Levi's
1973

104 **Advico-Delpire**
Levi's
1978

103 **Advico-Delpire**
Levi's
ca. 1973

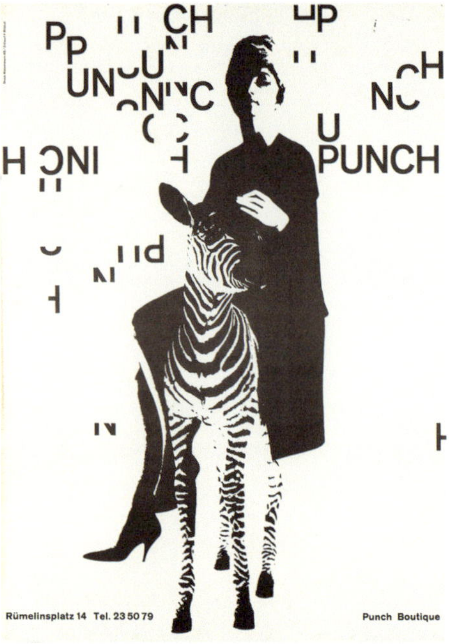

105 **George Tscherny**
San Francisco Clothing
1990

106 **Atelier-Galérie Kurt Strub**
Drake Store
1969

107 **P. Mitzkat**
Punch Boutique
1960

108 **Ruedi Walti**
Au père et fils
1986

109 **Jörg Schwerzmann**
Dschingis
1971

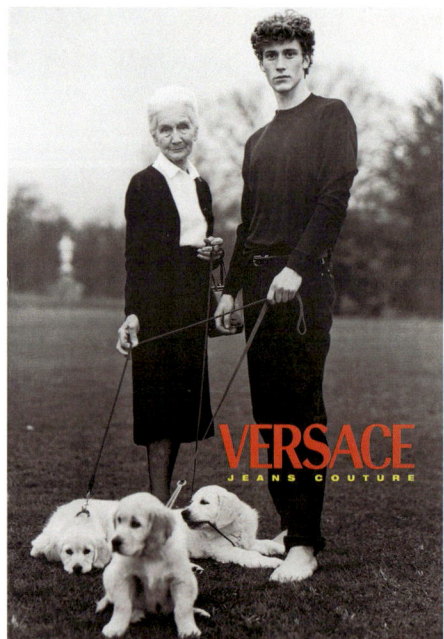

110 **Sulzer, Sutter**
Der neue Mann / Der neue PKZ
1992

111 **Anonym**
Hugo Boss
1998

112 **Hennes & Mauritz Marketing Department**
H&M / Pulli 29.90
1999

113 **Anonym**
Versace / Jeans Couture
1997

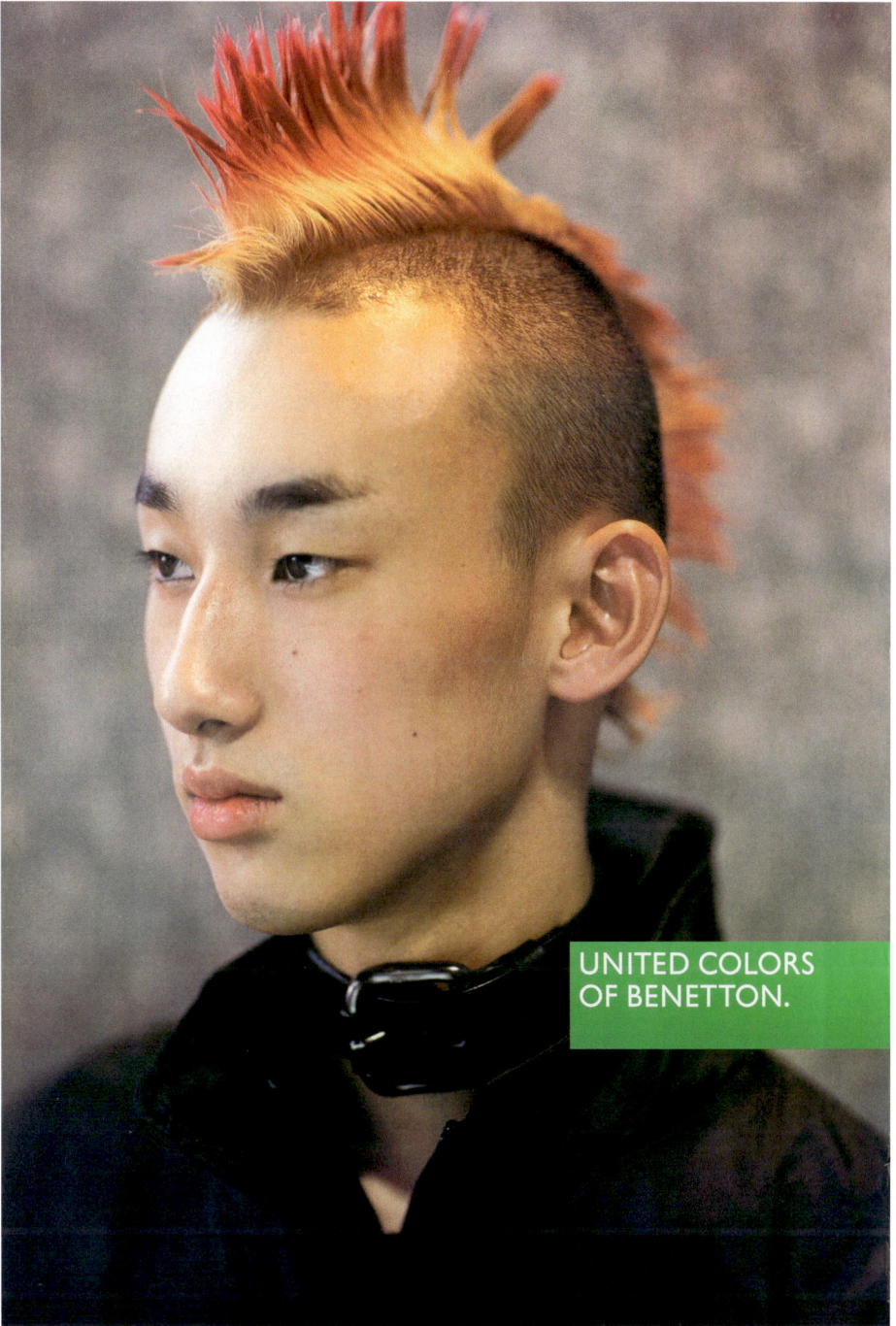

UNITED COLORS
OF BENETTON.

114 **Sisar**
United Colors of Benetton.
1999

115 **Oliviero Toscani**
I Want My Clothes Back / Empty Your Closets
1993

116 **Oliviero Toscani**
United Colors of Benetton.
1994

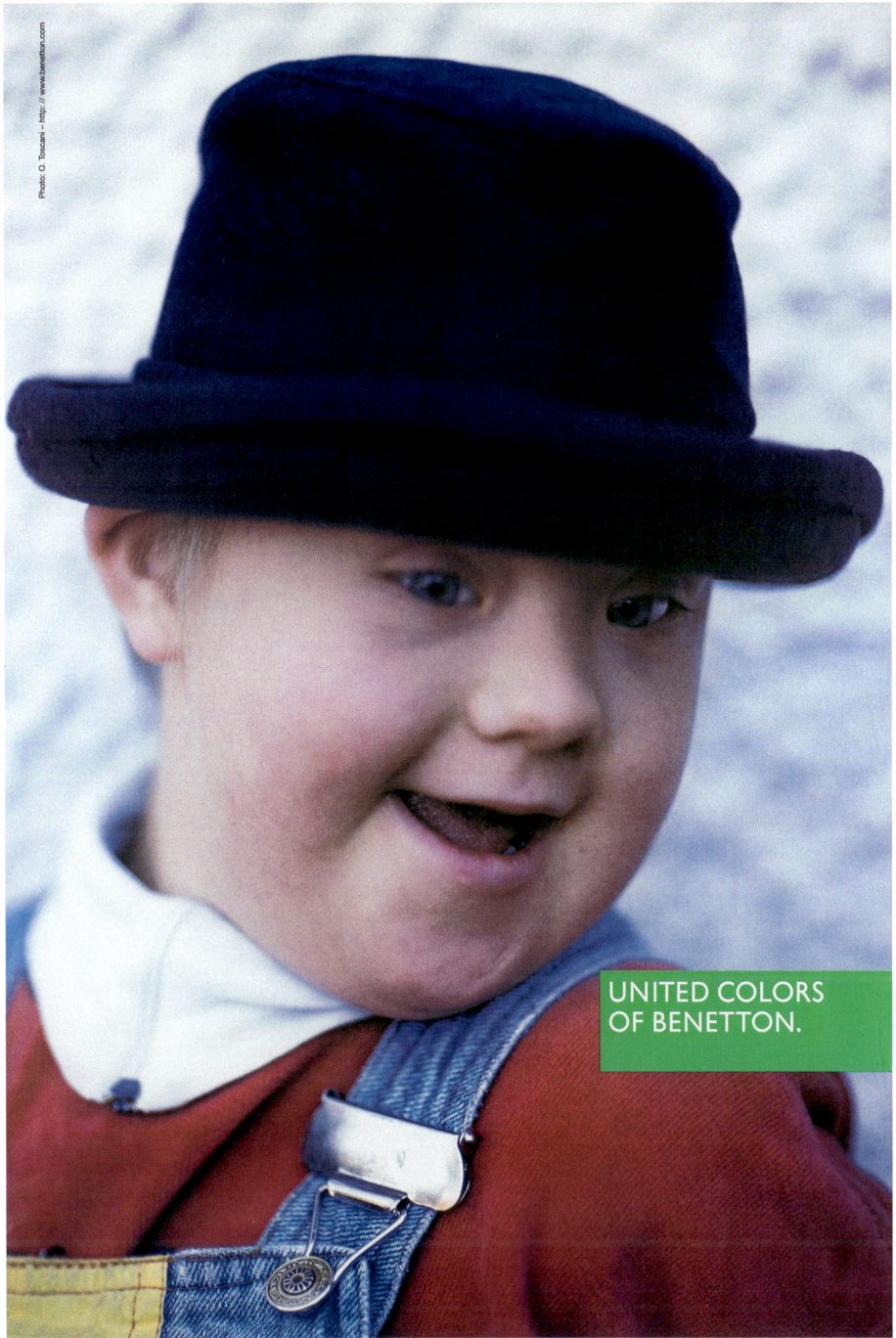

UNITED COLORS OF BENETTON.

117 **Salvatore Gregorietti, Oliviero Toscani**
United Colors of Benetton.
1998

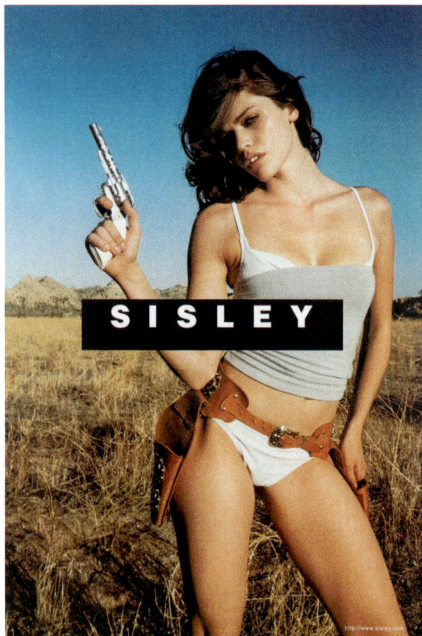

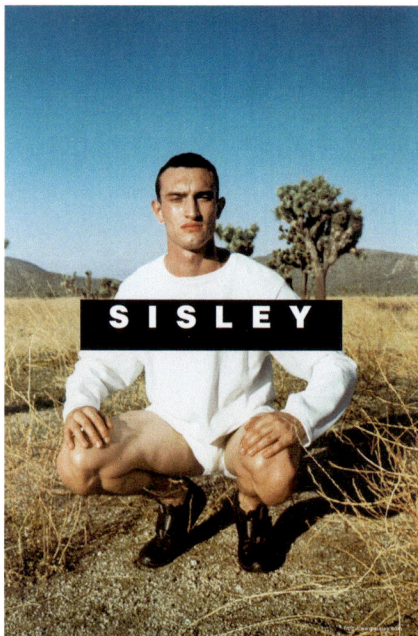

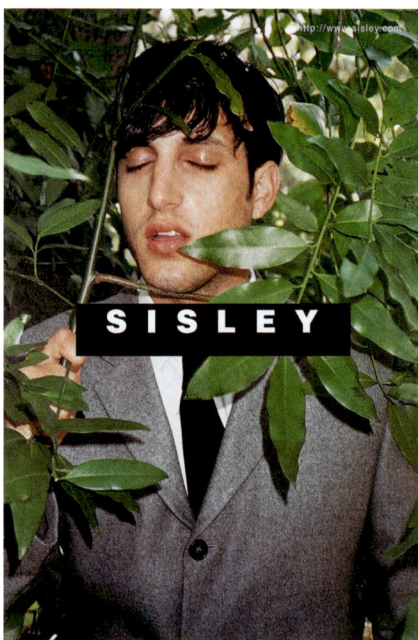

118 **Anonym**
Sisley
2000

119 **Anonym**
Sisley
1999

120 **Anonym**
Sisley
2000

121 **Anonym**
Sisley
1999

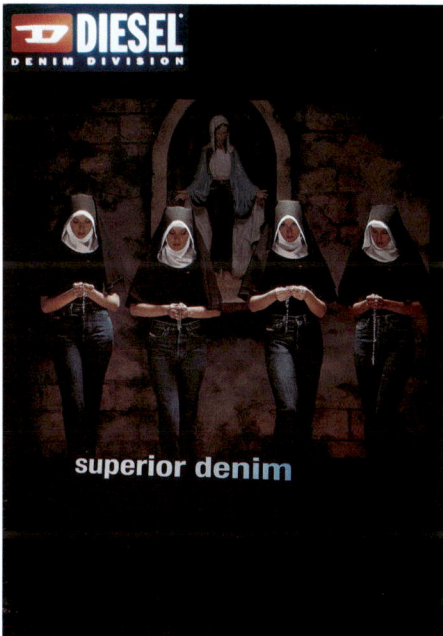

122 **Anonym**
Diesel
2008

123 **Anonym**
Diesel Denim Division
1998

124 **Anonym**
Diesel
2008

125 **Anonym**
Diesel
2007

126 **Bartle Bogle Hegarty / Mike Wells**
Levi's 517
1995

127 **Bartle Bogle Hegarty / Mike Wells**
Levi's 511
1995

128 **Anonym**
On The Wild Side
1995

129 **Bartle Bogle Hegarty / Mike Wells**
Levi's 518
1995

130 **Anonym**
Mustang
1995

Die Daten des Katalogs folgen den Rubriken Gestaltung,
Plakattext, Erscheinungsjahr, Erscheinungsland,
Drucktechnik, Format und Donationsnachweis. Dabei
gelten insbesondere folgende Regelungen:

Plakattext: Die beste Textwiedergabe bildet die Abbildung
des Plakates selbst. Darum wird hier eine vereinfachte
Form wiedergegeben, welche nur die aussagekräftigen
Textbestandteile berücksichtigt. Allfällige Umstellungen
dienen der Verständlichkeit. Das Zeichen / trennt in-
haltliche Texteinheiten. Jeweils in Klammern nachgestellt
folgt die deutsche und/oder englische Übersetzung.

Erscheinungsland: Das Erscheinungsland wird mit dem
international gebräuchlichen ISO-Code angegeben.

Format: Die Angaben werden in der Abfolge
Höhe × Breite und in cm gemacht. Weil die Plakate oft
nicht exakt rechtwinklig geschnitten sind, werden die
Abmessungen auf halbe cm aufgerundet.

Donationsnachweis: Die Geschichte der Plakatsammlung
geht auf das Jahr 1875 zurück. Angaben zur Herkunft
der Plakate sind in vielen Fällen nicht überliefert. Erst in
jüngerer Zeit werden Donatoren von Plakaten – Institutionen oder Einzelpersonen – konsequent festgehalten
und in Veröffentlichungen namentlich publiziert.

Die Plakatgeschichte ist ein junges Forschungsgebiet –
verlässliche Hinweise sind rar. Jeder Hinweis und jede
Ergänzung sind willkommen:
sammlungen@museum-gestaltung.ch

Catalogue

The data listed in the catalogue is broken down into the
following sections: designer, poster title and/or text,
year and country of first appearance, printing technique,
size, and donor. In particular, the following rules have
been applied:

Poster text: The poster itself provides the best version
of the text, and thus a simplified form is used which
provides only the most meaningful elements. Any
rearrangements that have been made are for purposes
of intelligibility. A slash mark separates textual units
by content. The German and/or English translation is
set in parentheses after the poster text.

Country of first appearance: The country of first
appearance is identified by the internationally accepted
ISO code.

Format: The dimensions are given in centimeters as
height × width. Because posters are often not cut exactly
at right angles, the dimensions are rounded off to the
half-centimeter.

Donor: The history of the Poster Collection goes back
to 1875. In many cases, we lack specific information
concerning the sources of posters in the collection.
Only recently have institutional or individual contributors
of posters been recorded consistently and specified in
our publications.

The history of posters is a recent field of research–
reliable information is rare. Any further references or
additional material are welcome:
sammlungen@museum-gestaltung.ch

1 Otto Baumberger (1889–1961)
Seiden-Grieder Zürich
1913 CH Lithografie – Lithograph
127 × 90 cm

2 Niklaus Stoecklin (1896–1982)
PKZ
1934 CH Lithografie – Lithograph
127 × 90 cm

3 Lora Lamm (*1928)
Photo: Serge Libiszewski (1930–2019)
La moda si diffonde con la Rinascente
(Die Mode verbreitet sich mit
La Rinascente – Fashion Spreads
with La Rinascente)
1959 IT Offset 100 × 70 cm
Donation Lora Lamm

4 Oliviero Toscani (*1942)
Photo: Oliviero Toscani (*1942)
United Colors of Benetton.
1992 Diverse Erscheinungsländer –
Various countries of first appearance
Offset 42 × 30 cm

5 Rikako Nagashima (*1980)
Dictionary / Mind of Telepathy
(Wörterbuch / Der Geist der Telepathie)
2010 JP Inkjet 103 × 73 cm
Donation Rikako Nagashima

6 Anonym
Sisley
2002 Diverse Erscheinungsländer –
Various countries of first appearance
Siebdruck – Screenprint 170 × 118 cm
Donation Allgemeine Plakatgesellschaft,
APG, Zürich

7 Hans Erni (1909–2015)
Seiden Grieder / Zürich / Luzern /
St. Moritz
1946 CH Lithografie – Lithograph
127 × 90 cm

8 Hans Falk (1918–2002)
Seiden Grieder / Zürich / St. Moritz /
Luzern
1950 CH Lithografie – Lithograph
127 × 90 cm

9 Charles Honoré Loupot (1892–1962)
Seiden-Grieder / Zürich
1918 CH Lithografie – Lithograph
128 × 90,5 cm

10 Hans Falk (1918–2002)
PKZ
1944 CH Lithografie – Lithograph
128 × 90,5 cm

11 Peter Birkhäuser (1911–1976)
PKZ
1934 CH Lithografie – Lithograph
127 × 90 cm

12 Wirz Werbung / Sandro Bocola
(*1931)
Photo: Max Emil Buchmann (1921–2014)
Die besten Stoffe der Welt verarbeitet
PKZ (PKZ Uses the World's Best
Fabrics)
1961 CH Offset 127 × 90 cm

13 Wirz Werbung / Sandro Bocola
(*1931)
Photo: Max Emil Buchmann (1921–2014)
Handarbeit hat hohe Geltung bei PKZ
(PKZ Values Excellent Needlework)
1961 CH Offset 127 × 90 cm

14 Hans Looser (1919–1988)
Tuch AG für erstklassige Verarbeitung
(Tuch AG for First-Rate Workmanship)
1961 CH Offset 127 × 90 cm

15 Otto Baumberger (1889–1961)
Marque PKZ
1923 CH Lithografie – Lithograph
128 × 90,5 cm

16 Stephan Krotowski (1881–1948)
Marke PKZ / Burger-Kehl & Co.
1913 CH Lithografie – Lithograph
131,5 × 98,5 cm
Donation Kunstmuseum Winterthur

17 Otto Morach (1887–1973)
Jedermann PKZ (Everyman PKZ)
1928 CH Lithografie – Lithograph
128 × 90,5 cm

18 Ludwig Hohlwein (1874–1949)
Marque PKZ
1908 CH Lithografie – Lithograph
128 × 93 cm

19 Herbert Matter (1907–1984)
PKZ
1928 CH Lithografie – Lithograph
128 × 90,5 cm

20 Viktor Rutz (1913–2008)
zugeschrieben / ascribed to
Pelz Kuhn / Elegante Pelzmäntel
(Pelz Kuhn / Elegant Fur Coats)
ca. 1932 CH Lithografie – Lithograph
127 × 90 cm

21 Masaaki Hiromura (*1954),
Takafumi Kusagaya (*1963)
Photo: Yutaka Satano
Miyake Design Studio / Necktie
(Miyake Design Studio / Krawatte)
1990 JP Offset 103 × 73 cm

22 Masaaki Hiromura (*1954),
Takafumi Kusagaya (*1963)
Photo: Yutaka Satano
Miyake Design Studio / Jackets
(Miyake Design Studio / Jacketts)
1990 JP Offset 103 × 73 cm

23 Masaaki Hiromura (*1954),
Takafumi Kusagaya (*1963)
Photo: Yutaka Satano
Miyake Design Studio / The Shirts
(Miyake Design Studio / Die Hemden)
1990 JP Offset 103 × 73 cm

24 Heini Fischer (1921–1990)
PKZ
1952 CH Offset 128 × 90,5 cm

25 Otto Baumberger (1889–1961)
PKZ zieht um (PKZ Is Moving)
1925 CH Lithografie – Lithograph
128 × 90,5 cm

26 Joseph Binder (1898–1972)
Der Jawo Mantel (The Jawo Overcoat)
1930 AT Lithografie – Lithograph
188 × 126 cm

27 Atelier Eidenbenz /
Hanspeter Rolly (1924–1994)
Tuch AG
1957 CH Lithografie – Lithograph
127 × 90 cm

28 Masaaki Hiromura (*1954),
Toshiyuki Kojima
Photo: Toshiaki Takeuchi (*1953)
Muji Hemden-Laden / Diverse
Grössen vorhanden / Tragen Sie ein
Hemd, das Ihrer Grösse entspricht /
Der Kragen, der sich um den Hals
und die Ärmel, die sich um die
Arme schmiegen, lassen sich leicht
ausdehnen und sind somit stets
bequem zu tragen / S, M, L, LL /
Geniessen Sie die anpassungsfähigen
Hemden in einer Vielzahl von
Grössen, Materialien und Formen
von Muji – Muji Shirt Store / Various
Sizes Available / Wear a shirt that
is just the right size for you / The
collar and sleeves fit snugly at the
neck and arms, yet stretch with ease,
ensuring comfortable wear at all
times / S, M, L, LL / Enjoy Muji's
adaptable shirts in a host of sizes,
materials and designs
1990 JP Offset 103 × 73 cm

29 Atelier Eidenbenz
Tuch AG / Gut in Form und Qualität
(Tuch AG / Good Design and Quality)
1948 CH Lithografie – Lithograph
127 × 90 cm

30 Elso Schiavo (*1934)
Photo: Max Roth (1923–2011)
Mode Zehnder
1972 CH Siebdruck – Screenprint
128 × 90,5 cm

31 Peter Birkhäuser (1911–1976)
Durable
1951 CH Lithografie – Lithograph
127 × 90 cm

32 K. D. Geissbühler (*1932)
Dschingis / Der Herrenausstatter im
Clipperhaus (Dschingis / The
Gentlemen's Outfitter at Clipperhaus)
1978 CH Siebdruck – Screenprint
127 × 90 cm

33 Roman Cieślewicz (1930–1996)
Moda Polska Warszawa (Polnische
Mode Warschau – Polish Fashion
Warsaw)
1959 PL Offset 68 × 48 cm

34 Salvatore Gregorietti (*1941)
Photo: Serge Libiszewski (1930–2019)
IR / Estate indiana (IR / Indian Summer)
1968 IT Offset 100 × 70 cm
Donation Serge Libiszewski

35 Transphère
Grieder Les Boutiques / «Spiel mit Stil»
(Grieder Les Boutiques /
"Playing with Style")
1997 CH Offset 128 × 90,5 cm
Donation Allgemeine Plakatgesellschaft,
APG, Zürich

36 Transphère
Bon Génie Les Boutiques / «Jeux
d'élégances» (Bon Génie Les Boutiques
/ «Spiel mit Eleganz» – Bon Génie Les
Boutiques / "Playing with Elegance")
1996 CH Offset 128 × 90,5 cm

37 Rogivue & Schmid
Barbados Jeans
1972 CH Offset 128 × 90,5 cm

38 Max Linder Werbeagentur / Peter
Christian Jost (*1938)
Photo: Peter Christian Jost (*1938),
Rolf Weiss (*1948)
Lee Cooper
1971 CH Offset 127 × 90cm

39 Amrein-Pieren
Ciolina / La Mode
1994 CH Siebdruck – Screenprint
128 × 90,5 cm

40 Amrein-Pieren
Ciolina / La Mode
1994 CH Siebdruck – Screenprint
128 × 90,5 cm

41 Lora Lamm (*1928)
La Rinascente / Estate e moda
(La Rinascente / Sommer und Mode –
La Rinascente / Summer and Fashion)
1958 IT Offset 70 × 100 cm

42 Lora Lamm (*1928)
IR / Apertura di stagione (IR /
Saisoneröffnung – IR / Season
Opening)
1957 IT Offset 100 × 70 cm
Donation Lora Lamm

43 Lora Lamm (*1928)
IR / La moda 1960 / Per la città,
i viaggi, la professione (IR / Mode 1960 /
Für die Stadt, die Reisen, die Arbeit –
IR / Fashion in 1960 / For Town,
Travel, Work)
1960 IT Offset 100 × 70 cm
Donation Lora Lamm

44 Lora Lamm (*1928)
La moda attuale è la confezione /
La confection régit la mode actuelle /
Today's Fashion Is Confection
(Heutige Mode ist Konfektion)
1959 IT Offset 100 × 70 cm
Donation Lora Lamm

45 Max Huber (1919–1992)
Per voi tutta la moda / È l'autunno della
Rinascente (Die ganze Mode für Sie /
Herbst bei La Rinascente – The Whole
World of Fashion for You / Autumn at La
Rinascente)
1954 IT Offset 70 × 100 cm

46 Max Huber (1919–1992)
La Rinascente / Moda autunno–inverno
1955 (La Rinascente / Herbst-
Winter-Mode 1955 – La Rinascente /
Autumn Winter Fashion 1955)
1955 IT Offset 70 × 100 cm

47–50 Atelier Hablützel und Jaquet /
Reinhart Morscher (1938–2004)
Löw Boutique
1975 CH Offset 128 × 90,5 cm

51 Christian Coigny (*1946)
Photo: Christian Coigny (*1946)
Grieder
1978 CH Siebdruck – Screenprint
127 × 90 cm

52 Christian Coigny (*1946)
Photo: Christian Coigny (*1946)
Grieder
1982 CH Siebdruck – Screenprint
128 × 90,5 cm
Donation Anton Erni

53 Christian Coigny (*1946)
Photo: Christian Coigny (*1946)
Grieder
1977 CH Siebdruck – Screenprint
127 × 90 cm

54 Christian Coigny (*1946)
Photo: Christian Coigny (*1946)
Grieder
1979 CH Siebdruck – Screenprint
127 × 90 cm

55 Christian Coigny (*1946)
Photo: Christian Coigny (*1946)
Grieder Les Boutiques
ca. 1983 CH Siebdruck – Screenprint
128 × 90,5 cm
Donation Anton Erni

56 Makoto Saito (*1952)
Jun Men
1986 JP Offset 103 × 145 cm

57 Jun Shibata (*1959)
Vivre / Probierst Du es bald an? –
Vivre / Are You Going to Try It
on Soon?
1992 JP Offset 103 × 145 cm

58 Masami Shimizu (*1953)
Vivre / Shopping muntert dich auf –
Vivre / Shopping Perks You up
1992 JP Offset 103 × 145 cm

59/60 Rhyner & Haettenschweiler /
Thomas Rhyner (*1961), Sasha
Haettenschweiler (*1969)
Photo: Christian Moser (*1963)
Pink Flamingo
1991 CH Siebdruck – Screenprint
128 × 90,5 cm
Donation René Grüninger PR, Zürich

61 Masami Shimizu (*1953)
Vivre / Möchtest Du einkaufen gehen?
– Vivre / Do You Want to Go
Shopping?
1992 JP Offset 103 × 145 cm

62 Takuya Onuki (*1958)
Laforet
1991 JP Offset 103 × 145 cm

63 Masami Shimizu (*1953)
Vivre / Soll ich etwas kaufen? –
Vivre / Should I Buy Something?
1992 JP Offset 103 × 145 cm

64 Takuya Onuki (*1958),
Yuichi Shimabayashi
Photo: Shintaro Shiratori
Laforet
1991 JP Offset 103 × 145 cm

65 M/M (Paris) / Michael Amzalag
(*1968), Mathias Augustyniak (*1967)
Photo: Inez van Lamsweerde (*1963),
Vinoodh Matadin (*1961)
S / The Alphabet / Stephanie Seymour
2001 FR Siebdruck – Screenprint
176 × 120,5 cm

66 M/M (Paris) / Michael Amzalag
(*1968), Mathias Augustyniak (*1967)
Photo: Inez van Lamsweerde (*1963),
Vinoodh Matadin (*1961)
W / The Alphabet / Veronica Webb
2001 FR Siebdruck – Screenprint
176 × 120,5 cm

67 M/M (Paris) / Michael Amzalag
(*1968), Mathias Augustyniak (*1967)
Photo: Inez van Lamsweerde (*1963),
Vinoodh Matadin (*1961)
V / The Alphabet / Guinevere van Seenus
2001 FR Siebdruck – Screenprint
176 × 120,5 cm

68 M/M (Paris) / Michael Amzalag
(*1968), Mathias Augustyniak (*1967)
Photo: Inez van Lamsweerde (*1963),
Vinoodh Matadin (*1961)
X / The Alphabet / Xeyenne
2001 FR Siebdruck – Screenprint
176 × 120,5 cm

69/70 Makoto Saito (*1952)
1986 Alpha Cubic
1986 JP Offset 103 × 145 cm

71 Nagi Noda (1973–2008)
Photo: Shoji Uchida (*1969)
Vivre / Mariko Takahashis Fitnessvideo
über «ein Mädchen, das mal fett war» /
Hallo, du erfreuliches, leidenschaft-
liches Vivre-Schnäppchen – Vivre /
Mariko Takahashi's Fitness Video
about "A Girl Who Used Fo Be Fat" /
Hello to Lovely, Exciting Bargains
2004 JP Offset 103 × 73 cm
Donation Takayuki Soeda

72 Nagi Noda (1973–2008)
Laforet / Happy Anniversary
(Laforet / Alles Gute zum Jahrestag)
2005 JP Offset 103 × 73 cm
Donation Takayuki Soeda

73 Tomoko Ikeda, Hiromi Oji,
Masami Shimizu (*1953)
Photo: Sachiko Kuru
Parco
1989 JP Offset 103 × 145 cm
Donation Graphis Verlag, Zürich

74 Draft Co.
Une nana cool
2003 JP Offset 103 × 145 cm
Donation Draft Co. Ltd., Tokio

75 Anonym
Diesel / Nature / Love It While It Lasts
(Diesel / Natur / Liebe sie, solange
es sie noch gibt)
2004 CH Offset 128 × 90,5 cm
Donation Allgemeine Plakatgesellschaft,
APG, Zürich

76 Makoto Saito (*1952)
Onward / The Global Staff of
Onward Presents a Highly Sensitive
International Brand for Contemporary
Fashion-Loving Women. (Onward /
Die Mitarbeiter von Onward präsen-
tieren eine hypersensitive Marke
für moderne, modeverrückte Frauen.)
1995 JP Offset 103 × 145 cm
Donation Graphis Verlag, Zürich

77 Christian Coigny (*1946),
Werner Jeker (*1944)
Photo: Christian Coigny (*1946)
Grieder Les Boutiques
1986 CH Siebdruck – Screenprint
128 × 90,5 cm
Donation Anton Erni

78 Christian Coigny (*1946)
Photo: Christian Coigny (*1946)
Grieder Les Boutiques
1984 CH Siebdruck – Screenprint
128 × 90,5 cm
Donation Anton Erni

79 Transphère
Grieder Brunschwig Group /
Eleganz, unser Stil (Grieder Brunschwig
Group / Elegance, Our Style)
2008 CH Offset 170 × 118 cm
Donation Allgemeine Plakatgesellschaft,
APG, Zürich

80 Christian Coigny (*1946)
Photo: Christian Coigny (*1946)
Grieder Les Boutiques
1985 CH Siebdruck – Screenprint
128 × 90,5 cm

81 Ikko Tanaka (1930–2002)
Photo: Irving Penn (1917–2009)
Issey Miyake 1999
1999 JP Offset 103 × 73 cm
Donation DNP Foundation for Cultural
Promotion, Tokio und Kabushiki Kaisha
Tanaka Ikko Design Shitsu, Tokio

82 Ikko Tanaka (1930–2002)
Photo: Irving Penn (1917–2009)
Issey Miyake 1999
1999 JP Offset 103 × 73 cm
Donation DNP Foundation for Cultural
Promotion, Tokio und Kabushiki Kaisha
Tanaka Ikko Design Shitsu, Tokio

83 Ikko Tanaka (1930–2002)
Photo: Irving Penn (1917–2009)
Issey Miyake 1998
1998 JP Offset 103 × 73 cm
Donation DNP Foundation for Cultural
Promotion, Tokio und Kabushiki Kaisha
Tanaka Ikko Design Shitsu, Tokio

84 Ikko Tanaka (1930–2002)
Photo: Francis Giacobetti (*1939)
Issey Miyake / Making Things
2000 JP Offset 103 × 73 cm
Donation DNP Foundation for Cultural
Promotion, Tokio und Kabushiki Kaisha
Tanaka Ikko Design Shitsu, Tokio

85/86 Makoto Saito (*1952)
Alpha Cubic
1990 JP Offset 103 × 145 cm

87 Makoto Saito (*1952)
Ba-Tsu 1994 / Harajuku / Tokyo
1994 JP Offset 103 × 145 cm

88 Makoto Saito (*1952)
Alpha Cubic 95
1995 JP Siebdruck – Screenprint
136 × 103 cm

89 Makoto Saito (*1952),
Eiichiro Sakata (*1941)
Alpha Cubic
1988 JP Siebdruck – Screenprint
103 × 145 cm

90 Makoto Saito (*1952)
Alpha Cubic 1987
1987 JP Offset 103 × 145 cm

91 Makoto Saito (*1952)
Kind Wear
1989 JP Offset 145 × 103 cm

92 Makoto Saito (*1952)
Kind Wear
1989 JP Siebdruck – Screenprint
103 × 145 cm

93 Makoto Saito (*1952)
0001 Alpha Cubic
1988 JP Siebdruck – Screenprint
103 × 145 cm

94 Makoto Saito (*1952)
1992 / Kind Wear / Bulbs. Tubers.
(1992 / Kind Wear / Zwiebeln. Knollen.)
1992 JP Offset 108,5 × 153 cm

95/96 Makoto Saito (*1952)
1985 Alpha Cubic
1985 JP Siebdruck – Screenprint
103 × 145 cm

97 Makoto Saito (*1952)
Alpha Cubic for Joseph Beuys
1984 JP Offset 103 × 145 cm

98 Makoto Saito (*1952)
Kind Wear
1988 JP Offset 103 × 145 cm

99 Sagmeister / Joe Shouldice (*1975),
Richard The (*1980)
Photo: Tom Schierlitz (1959–2018)
This Is a Pair of Levi's Sewed
with the Strongest Thread
(Das ist ein Paar Levi's, genäht
mit den stärksten Faden)
2008 US Siebdruck – Screenprint
119 × 84,5 cm
Donation C2F, Luzern

100 Sagmeister / Joe Shouldice
(*1975), Richard The (*1980)
Photo: Tom Schierlitz (1959–2018)
[ohne Text – no text]
2008 US Siebdruck – Screenprint
119 × 84,5 cm
Donation C2F, Luzern

101 Peter Marti (*1954)
Rifle Traumjeans (Rifle Dream Jeans)
1982 CH Offset 128 × 90,5 cm
Donation Kloster Einsiedeln

102 Advico-Delpire
Levi's
1973 CH Offset 98,5 × 66 cm

103 Advico-Delpire
Levi's
ca. 1973 CH Offset 66 × 98,5 cm

104 Advico-Delpire
Levi's
1978 CH Offset 92 × 62 cm

105 George Tscherny (*1924)
San Francisco Clothing
1990 US Siebdruck – Screenprint
98 × 66 cm
Donation George Tscherny

106 Atelier-Galérie Kurt Strub
Drake Store / Boutique for Men
1969 CH Offset 128 × 90,5 cm

107 P. Mitzkat
Punch / Punch Boutique
1960 CH Offset 128 × 90,5 cm

108 Ruedi Walti (*1957)
Photo: Monique Delley
Au père et fils / Mode masculine
(Für Vater und Sohn / Männermode –
For Father and Son / Menswear)
1986 CH Siebdruck – Screenprint
128 × 90,5 cm

109 Jörg Schwerzmann (*1943)
Dschingis
1971 CH Offset 127 × 90 cm
Donation Allgemeine Plakatgesellschaft,
APG, Zürich

110 Sulzer, Sutter
Der neue Mann / Der neue PKZ
(The New Man / The New PKZ)
1992 CH Offset 170 × 118 cm

111 Anonym
Hugo Boss
1998 Diverse Erscheinungsländer –
Various countries of first appearance
Offset 170 × 118 cm

112 Hennes & Mauritz Marketing
Department
H&M / Pulli 29.90
1999 Diverse Erscheinungsländer –
Various countries of first appearance
Offset 170 × 118 cm
Donation Allgemeine Plakatgesellschaft,
APG, Zürich

113 Anonym
Versace / Jeans Couture
1997 Diverse Erscheinungsländer –
Various countries of first appearance
Offset 170 × 118 cm
Donation Allgemeine Plakatgesellschaft,
APG, Zürich

114 Sisar
Photo: Oliviero Toscani (*1942)
United Colors of Benetton.
1999 Diverse Erscheinungsländer –
Various countries of first appearance
Offset 170 × 118 cm

115 Oliviero Toscani (*1942)
I Want My Clothes Back / Empty
Your Closets / Redistribution Project
Donated by the Clients of United
Colors of Benetton. (Gebt mir meine
Kleider zurück / Leert eure Kleider-
schränke / Ein Umverteilungsprojekt
gespendet von den Kunden von
United Colors of Benetton.)
1993 Diverse Erscheinungsländer –
Various countries of first appearance
Offset 30 × 42 cm

116 Oliviero Toscani (*1942)
Photo: Oliviero Toscani (*1942)
United Colors of Benetton.
1994 Diverse Erscheinungsländer –
Various countries of first appearance
Offset 30 × 42 cm

117 Salvatore Gregorietti (*1941),
Oliviero Toscani (*1942)
Photo: Oliviero Toscani (*1942)
United Colors of Benetton.
1998 Diverse Erscheinungsländer –
Various countries of first appearance
Offset 170 × 118 cm

118 Anonym
Sisley
2000 Diverse Erscheinungsländer –
Various countries of first appearance
Offset 170 × 118 cm
Donation Allgemeine Plakatgesellschaft,
APG, Zürich

119 Anonym
Sisley
1999 Diverse Erscheinungsländer –
Various countries of first appearance
Offset 170 × 118 cm

120 Anonym
Sisley
2000 Diverse Erscheinungsländer –
Various countries of first appearance
Offset 170 × 118 cm
Donation Allgemeine Plakatgesellschaft,
APG, Zürich

121 Anonym
Sisley
1999 Diverse Erscheinungsländer –
Various countries of first appearance
Offset 170 × 118 cm

122 Anonym
Diesel / Live Fast (Lebe schnell)
2008 Diverse Erscheinungsländer –
Various countries of first appearance
Offset 170 × 118 cm
Donation Allgemeine Plakatgesellschaft,
APG, Zürich

123 Anonym
Diesel Denim Division / Superior Denim
1998 Diverse Erscheinungsländer –
Various countries of first appearance
Offset 170 × 118 cm
Donation Allgemeine Plakatgesellschaft,
APG, Zürich

124 Anonym
Diesel / Live Fast (Lebe schnell)
2008 Diverse Erscheinungsländer –
Various countries of first appearance
Offset 170 × 118 cm
Donation Allgemeine Plakatgesellschaft,
APG, Zürich

125 Anonym
Diesel / Global Warming Ready (Diesel
/ Bereit für die globale Erwärmung)
2007 Diverse Erscheinungsländer –
Various countries of first appearance
Offset 170 × 118 cm
Donation Allgemeine Plakatgesellschaft,
APG, Zürich

126 Bartle Bogle Hegarty / Mike Wells
Photo: Bill Brandt (1904–1983)
Levi's 517 / Regular Fit
1995 GB Offset 44 × 29 cm
Donation Graphis Verlag, Zürich

127 Bartle Bogle Hegarty / Mike Wells
Photo: Bill Brandt (1904–1983)
Levi's 511 / Zip Fly
1995 GB Offset 44 × 29 cm
Donation Graphis Verlag, Zürich

128 Anonym
On the Wild Side
1995 CH Offset 128 × 90,5 cm
Donation Allgemeine Plakatgesellschaft,
APG, Zürich

129 Bartle Bogle Hegarty / Mike Wells
Photo: Bill Brandt (1904–1983)
Levi's 518 / Loose Fit
1995 GB Offset 44 × 29 cm
Donation Graphis Verlag, Zürich

130 Anonym
Mustang / On the Wild Side
1995 CH Offset 128 × 90,5 cm
Donation Allgemeine Plakatgesellschaft,
APG, Zürich

Ausgewählte Literatur / Selected Bibliography

Allenspach, Christoph, «Räume der Kleider. Inszenierung von sinnlichen Modewelten», in: Anna-Brigitte Schlittler, Katharina Tietze (eds.), *Kleider in Räumen,* Winterthur 2009, pp. 54–59.

Barthes, Roland, *Die Sprache der Mode,* Frankfurt a. M. 1985 (first edition: Paris 1967).

Baudelaire, Charles, «Der Maler des modernen Lebens», in: id., *Aufsätze zur Literatur und Kunst 1857–1860,* München 1989, pp. 213–258 (first edition: Paris 1860).

Bieger, Laura, Annika Reich, Susanne Rohr (eds.), *Mode. Ein kulturwissenschaftlicher Grundriss,* München 2012.

Boltanski, Luc, Ève Chiapello, «Die Arbeit der Kritik und der normative Wandel», in: Christoph Menke, Juliane Rebentisch (eds.), *Kreation und Depression. Freiheit im gegenwärtigen Kapitalismus,* Berlin 2019, pp. 18–37.

Bovenschen, Silvia (ed.), *Die Listen der Mode,* Frankfurt a. M. 1986.

Bruzzi, Stella, Pamela Church Gibson, *Fashion Cultures Revisited,* London 2013.

Bruzzi, Stella, Pamela Church Gibson, *Fashion Cultures. Theories, Explorations and Analysis,* London 2001.

Capa, Cornell (ed.), *The Concerned Photographer. The Photographs of Werner Bischof, André Kertész, Robert Capa, Leonard Freed, David Seymour («Chim»), Dan Weiner,* New York 1968.

Eismann, Sonja (ed.), *Absolute Fashion,* Freiburg 2012.

Entwistle, Joanne, *The Fashioned Body. Fashion, Dress and Modern Social Theory,* second edition, Cambridge 2015.

Gaugele, Elke, Monica Titton (eds.), *Fashion and Postcolonial Critique,* Berlin 2019.

Goffman, Erving, *Geschlecht und Werbung,* Frankfurt a. M. 1981 (first edition: London 1979).

Graw, Isabelle, «Der letzte Schrei. Über modeförmige Kunst und kunstförmige Mode», in: *Texte zur Kunst,* vol. 14, no. 56, 2004, pp. 80–95.

Hug, Cathérine, Christoph Becker (eds.), *Fashion Drive. Extreme Mode in der Kunst,* exhib. cat., Kunsthaus Zürich, Bielefeld 2018.

Huster, Gabriele, *Wilde Frische – Zarte Versuchung. Männer- und Frauenbild auf Werbeplakaten der fünfziger bis neunziger Jahre,* Marburg 2001.

Kawamura, Yuniya, *The Japanese Revolution in Paris Fashion,* Oxford 2004.

König, René, *Menschheit auf dem Laufsteg. Die Mode im Zivilisationsprozess,* München/Wien 1985.

Kubasiewicz, Jan, Makoto Saito, «Reputations: Makoto Saito», in: *Eye,* vol. 9, no. 35, 2000.

Lehnert, Gertrud (ed.), *Mode, Weiblichkeit und Modernität,* Dortmund 1998.

Lehnert, Gertrud, *Mode. Theorie, Geschichte und Ästhetik einer kulturellen Praxis,* Bielefeld 2013.

Mitchell, W. J. T., *What Do Pictures Want? The Lives and Loves of Images,* Chicago 2006.

Nieder, Alison A., Jim Heimann, *20th Century Fashion. 100 Years of Apparel Ads,* second edition, Köln 2016.

Okakura, Kakuzō, *Das Buch vom Tee,* Frankfurt a. M. / Leipzig 1989 (first edition: New York 1906).

Richter, Bettina, «Zeitgenössische ‹Bilderstürmer›» / «Contemporary ‹Iconoclasts›», in: Museum für Gestaltung Zürich, Bettina Richter (eds.), *Help!,* Poster Collection 20, Baden 2009, pp. 64–65, 70–71.

Schmid, Helmut, *Japan japanisch – die leise Schönheit japanischer Dinge,* Tokio 2012.

Siegrist, Hannes, Hartmut Kaelble, Jürgen Kocka (eds.), *Europäische Konsumgeschichte – Zur Gesellschafts- und Kulturgeschichte des Konsums (18. bis 20. Jahrhundert),* Frankfurt a. M. / New York 1997.

Ullrich, Wolfgang, *Habenwollen. Wie funktioniert die Konsumkultur?,* Frankfurt a. M. 2006.

Veblen, Thorstein, *Theorie der feinen Leute. Eine ökonomische Untersuchung der Institutionen,* Frankfurt a. M. 2007 (first edition: New York / London 1899).

Vinken, Barbara, *Mode nach der Mode. Kleid und Geist am Ende des 20. Jahrhunderts,* Frankfurt a. M. 1993.

Autoren / Authors

Bettina Richter

Geboren 1964, Kunsthistorikerin. 1996 Dissertation über die Antikriegsgrafiken von Théophile-Alexandre Steinlen. 1997–2006 wissenschaftliche Mitarbeiterin in der Plakat-sammlung des Museum für Gestaltung Zürich. Seit 2006 Kuratorin der Plakatsammlung. Nebenbei Tätigkeit als Dozentin an der Zürcher Hochschule der Künste sowie als freischaffende Autorin.

Born 1964, art historian. Dissertation on the antiwar graphics of Théophile-Alexandre Steinlen, 1996. Served as research associate for the Poster Collection of the Museum für Gestaltung Zürich, 1997–2006, as curator since 2006. Also lectures at Zurich University of the Arts and works as a freelance writer.

Elke Gaugele

Empirische Kulturwissenschaftlerin und Professorin an der Akademie der bildenden Künste in Wien. Sie ist Leiterin des Fachbereich «Moden und Styles» und des Austrian Center for Fashion Research und Mitglied im DFG-Netzwerk «Entangled Histories of Art and Migration: Forms, Visibilities, Agents» (2018–2021). Aktuelle Publikationen: *Fashion and Postcolonial Critique* (hg. mit Monica Titton), Berlin / New York 2019; *Fashion as Politics: Dressing Dissent* (hg. mit Monica Titton), Sonderheft von *Fashion Theory. The Journal of Dress, Body and Culture,* vol. 24, 2019; *Critical Studies. Kultur- und Sozialtheorie im Kunstfeld* (hg. mit Jens Kastner), Wiesbaden 2016; *Aesthetic Politics in Fashion,* Berlin / New York 2014.

Cultural anthropologist and professor at the Academy of Fine Arts in Vienna. She heads the Fashion and Styles Department and the Austrian Center for Fashion Research. In addition, she is a member of the DFG network "Entangled Histories of Art and Migration: Forms, Visibi-lities, Agents" (2018–2021). Recent publications: *Fashion and Postcolonial Critique,* ed. with Monica Titton (Berlin / New York, 2019); *Fashion as Politics: Dressing Dissent,* ed. with Monica Titton, special issue of *Fashion Theory: The Journal of Dress, Body and Culture,* vol. 24 (2019); *Critical Studies: Kultur- und Sozialtheorie im Kunstfeld,* ed. with Jens Kastner (Wiesbaden, 2016); *Aesthetic Politics in Fashion* (Berlin / New York, 2014).

Dank / Acknowledgments

Publikations- und Ausstellungsprojekte sind immer ein willkommener Anlass, den eigenen, umfangreichen Bestand an Plakaten themenspezifisch zu sichten, aufzuarbeiten und zu ergänzen. Für die vorliegende Publikation konnten wir auf viele Plakatklassiker zurückgreifen, die der Sammlung im Verlauf ihrer Geschichte als Donation übergeben wurden. Für das uns geschenkte Vertrauen ebenso wie für Anregungen und Informationen zum Thema möchten wir uns an dieser Stelle ganz herzlich bedanken.

Publication and exhibition projects are always welcome occasions to examine and work with our own extensive holdings of posters with a specific theme in mind, and also to update it with targeted acquisitions. For this publication we were able to draw on numerous classic posters that have been donated to the collection over the course of its history. We would like to use this opportunity to express our sincere thanks for the trust placed in us and for the suggestions and information on the topic.

Museum
für Gestaltung
Zürich

Eine Publikation des Museum für Gestaltung Zürich
Christian Brändle, Direktor

A Publication of the Museum für Gestaltung Zürich
Christian Brändle, Director

En Vogue
Konzept und Redaktion / Concept and editing: Bettina Richter,
Barbara Schenkel, Petra Schmid
Gestaltung / Design: Integral Lars Müller
Übersetzung / Translation: Helen Ferguson (Ger.–Eng.)
Lektorat Deutsch / German copyediting: Markus Zehentbauer
Lektorat Englisch / English copyediting: Adam Blauhut
Fotografie / Photography: Ivan Suta
Lithografie / Repro: prints professional, Berlin, Germany
Druck, Einband / Printing, binding: Belvédère, Oosterbeek,
the Netherlands

Reihe / Series «Poster Collection»
Herausgegeben von / Edited by
Museum für Gestaltung Zürich, Plakatsammlung
Bettina Richter, Kuratorin der Plakatsammlung /
Curator of the Poster Collection
In Zusammenarbeit mit / In cooperation with
Petra Schmid, Publikationen / Publications
Museum für Gestaltung Zürich

Z The museum of
Zurich University of the Arts
zhdk.ch

Museum für Gestaltung Zürich
Ausstellungsstrasse 60
Postfach
8031 Zürich, Switzerland
www.museum-gestaltung.ch

Museum für Gestaltung Zürich
Plakatsammlung / Poster Collection
sammlungen@museum-gestaltung.ch

Lars Müller Publishers
8005 Zürich, Switzerland
www.lars-mueller-publishers.com

ISBN 978-3-03778-641-3
Erste Auflage / First edition

Printed in the Netherlands

Wir danken für Unterstützung /
For their support we thank:

⣤ APG|SGA

POSTER COLLECTION

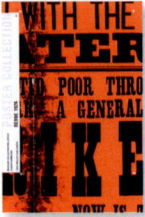
01 **REVUE 1926**

02 **DONALD BRUN**

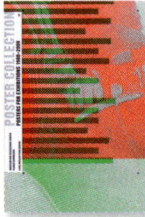
03 **POSTERS FOR EXHIBITIONS 1980–2000**

04 **HORS-SOL**

05 **TYPOTECTURE**

06 **VISUAL STRATEGIES AGAINST AIDS**

07 **ARMIN HOFMANN**

08 **BLACK AND WHITE**

09 **RALPH SCHRAIVOGEL**

10 **MICHAEL ENGELMANN**

11 **HANDMADE**

12 **CATHERINE ZASK**

13 **TYPO CHINA**

14 **ZÜRICH–MILANO**

15 **BREAKING THE RULES**

16 **COMIX!**

17 **PHOTO GRAPHICS**

18 **OTTO BAUMBERGER**

19 **HEAD TO HEAD**

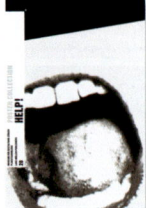
20 **HELP!**

21 **PARADISE SWITZERLAND**

22 **LETTERS ONLY**

23 **IN SERIES**

24 **THE MAGIC OF THINGS**

25 **JOSEF MÜLLER-BROCKMANN**

26 **JAPAN–NIPPON**

27 **THE HAND**

28 **HERBERT LEUPIN**

29 **HAMBURGER-STAEHELIN**

30 **SELF-PROMOTION**

31 **STOP MOTION**